# SCHOENBERG

TO THE LATE ALBAN BERG

EDITED BY M

# SCHOE

ARTICLES BY ARNOLD SCHOENBERG ▪ ERWIN STEIN ▪ CÉSAR SAERCHINGER ▪ ROGER SESSIONS ▪ CARL ENGEL ▪ LOUIS DANZ ▪ FRANZ WERFEL ▪ OTTO KLEMPERER ▪ NICHOLAS SLONIMSKY ▪ ERNST KRENEK ▪ RICHARD BUHLIG ▪ PAUL STEFAN ▪ BORIS de SCHLOEZER ▪ EDUARD STEUERMANN ▪ JOSÉ RODRIGUEZ ▪ PAUL AMADEUS PISK ▪ ADOLPH WEISS ▪ BERTHOLD VIERTEL ▪ MERLE ARMITAGE ▪ 1929 TO 1937

L E  A R M I T A G E

N B E R G

FOREWORD BY LEOPOLD STOKOWSKI ▪ AFFIRMATIONS BY ARNOLD SCHOENBERG ▪ A BIBLIOGRAPHY OF SCHOENBERG WORKS ▪ PORTRAITS BY EDWARD WESTON AND GEORGE GERSHWIN ▪ A SELF PORTRAIT BY ARNOLD SCHOENBERG ▪ CANDID CAMERA PHOTOGRAPHS BY OTTO ROTHSCHILD AND TWO INK DRAWINGS BY CARLOS DYER ▪

 **BOOKS FOR LIBRARIES PRESS**
**FREEPORT, NEW YORK**

INTERNATIONAL STANDARD BOOK NUMBER:
0-8369-5783-0


LIBRARY OF CONGRESS CATALOG CARD NUMBER:
77-157360


PRINTED IN THE UNITED STATES OF AMERICA

# C O N T E N T S

# CONTENTS

# FOREWORD

*Schönberg* stands alone. In the evolution of occidental music there never has been a musician of similar character and gifts. It may be long before his contribution to Music will be understood. Just as Leonardo da Vinci and Cézanne searched unceasingly for newly perceived truth in color and form, and interpretation on a two-dimensional surface of three-dimensional space, so Schönberg has enormously enlarged the tonal resources of tempered intervals and scale. In melodic line, harmony, counterpart, rhythm, flexibility and subtlety of counter-rhythms, balance, structure and relief of essential and dominating notes in harmony, he has been unendingly creative and courageous. Through his imagination he sees the today and tomorrow of the art to which he has devoted his life, and so is a true leader in the world of Music.

[1937]

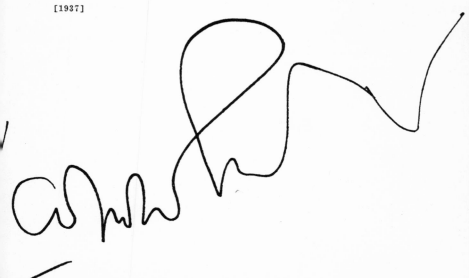

# MERLE ARMITAGE

This is an uncrystalized age. Former standards, even the old bulwarks of measurement, are gone. It is essentially a time of transition; the world is unresolved. Every element of swift change is manifest. The decline of an older culture, the rise of a new world-form, the insistence of manifold new attitudes, the presence of clashing incongruities, all are irrefutable evidence.

The most apparent and significant symptom is man's present pre-occupation with experimentation. The serenity of the past has given way to doubt and unbelief, which in turn has inspired and animated research. Much of the turmoil is a sign that the new tendencies are not yet strong enough to overthrow the old, creating thereby a tension, until through pressure, one after another the old ideas give way.

There is a quickening of pace in the manner of water accelerating as it approaches the rapids; the whirlpools

1

of chaos being an inevitable condition to attaining the serenity beyond.

Among the obvious products of this frenzy is the multiplicity of contradictions. Our time is productive of profound thought and of superficiality, of advanced liberality and smug reaction. The guiding lines of experience, the old foundations, much that was held sound, crumbles as it is subjected to modern scrutiny. Philosophy faces a panorama of riddles. All paths towards the future are tentative and vague. If staticity was representative of certain great dynasties in China and if individualization and refinement characterized the great days of Greece, and if creativeness was characteristic of the Renaissance, this is the undoubted age of transition.

Every cycle has had its pattern. Certain special themes have coursed through and become at one with each period. Inextricably are the activities of each epoch woven together. These may be called the design, the pattern, or the form of that epoch. By observing the art of each period in history, one can reconstruct the thought and the dominating motives and powers of that time.

**2**

Modern music knows no repose. Its creators are searching for new forms, selecting, observing, sometimes groping.

Concentration on pure music is not necessarily a product of our day. It has occured before, it has a periodic reoccurance whenever a deadlock occurs, or when there is a confused sense of direction. Yet a confused age may be one of great hopefulness and potentialities.

Whatever one's attitude may be towards the radical musical tendencies of today, and whatever in the final analysis may be the absolute value of contemporary composition, in considering the manifold evidences, no one can doubt that we are on the threshold of a profound change in musical art, which may lead to the practical application of a more subtle scale and to the embracing of a scale which is tonally more complicated.

Inasmuch as our diatonic scale was not established immediately, nor was the chromatic scale, the adoption of the new, whatever it may ultimately be, is forthrightly expected.

The more prudent composers have not attempted to

3

proceed contrary to the laws governing present day transition. There are no eternally finished works. Ignorance of these laws has caused some modern composers to seek a solution of the problem by shortcuts.

The basis of modern music is in direct opposition to romanticism. In their search for the esthetic formula of our time, composers have not and should not be bound by theories. Contemporary music is, in a sense, mathematically ordered anarchy. Yet we know the truth of Schoenberg's statements that ''The alleged tones believed to be foreign to harmony do not exist; they are merely tones foreign to our accepted harmonic system.'' ''Tonality is not a hard and fast compulsion directing the course of music but a concept which makes it possible for us to give our ideas the requisite aspect of compactness.''

The route into the future is via experimentation and research.

Research not being founded on ecstasy, the contemporary artist grapples with the essential qualities of things. The laws for instance, which governed transpor-

4

tation in the past, that is, travel on land and water, are not applicable to transport by air, yet both provide means of travel. Out of the diversity of idioms, the contradictions, and the false starts of modern music, emerges Schoenberg. The experimental impetus which he has imparted to music has not yet attained a full maturity. But he has created forms new to the structure of music and in the process of his mathematical-musical progress he may be said to have evolved or invented an entirely *new* method of writing or creating music.

Lesser men in music have fallen victim to the subsidiary, not the main currents, of our time. In their attempt to furnish purely social issues with a corresponding music, they have accepted the social theories in which they are immersed, exactly as in a more serene age they would consciously or unconsciously have been influenced by the systems and the idioms of other composers. This is impossible to the pioneer; to men of expanding ideas, and robust creative impulses.

Schoenberg occupies a position wholly alien to the ruffled surface waves of his generation, but entirely at one with its great ground swell; its significant ebb and flow.

The beauty of much of Schoenberg's music is austere. Its scholarly background, its mathematical, constellation-like form, its startling abridgments, its penetration, regardless of the pitfalls for habit-trained ears, yet achieves a peak of exultation and conjuration not encountered in the work of any living composer organized in Schoenberg's direction.

In this volume the phenomenon of Schoenberg is approached from many different view-points and attitudes. The very admission of an art and a world in flux, makes this an inevitable condition.

There is a freedom from the malady of much contemporary criticism, which only offers impressions, when the demand is for opinion.

The reader will encounter a certain elasticity in the use and application of musical terms hitherto regarded as stable and constant, due to the relative newness of ideas and approach. Further, it may appear that in the disagreements on the part of the various contributors,

6

there is no community of agreement and thought. Yet considered as a unit the book ultimately reflects an agreement wherein the dissonance of ideas resolves, and the progression of modern music plus Schoenberg's monumental contribution to it, are both clarified.

[1936]

**7**

# ROGER SESSIONS

There can no longer be any question that music, like every other manifestation of Western culture, stands under the sign of crisis. The situation has been developing for decades; nearly a century ago the most sensitive observers were already aware that some such crisis was approaching. But what has, until recently, been visible only to the most far-flung spirits has since the war become an increasingly obvious and menacing fact, with the most concrete and actual implications. The reactionary tendency observable in every country during the past two musical seasons is only the latest and one of the most superficial symptoms of an underlying condition; though its intrinsic importance must not be over-estimated, it is obviously the reaction of a public which for the first time in musical history feels itself increasingly out of touch, not with this or that contemporary composer, but with "modern music" itself.

The active musical tendencies of the past ten years have all been, in their several ways, efforts in the directions of meeting this crisis. In speaking of them it should never be forgotten that the development of art is a living, organic process, not to be defined accurately in terms of "movements," "reactions," and "tendencies." Such definitions are for the most part approximations adopted, with a rather deadly concreteness, not by protagonists but by spectators; in order to understand what is really happening one must get behind the definitions to facts, which then must be viewed in perspective. Such formulas have their practical usefulness, no doubt; but they have also the fundamental falseness of all attempts to classify matter which is stubbornly alive and constantly developing.

One must exercise a certain caution, moreover, in regard to the utterances of composers themselves. The creative activity is essentially practical rather than theoretical, and like all practical natures the artist is necessarily absorbed in his own problems, even though occasionally, as in the case for instance of Wagner, he is capable of making vital generalizations as well. But impersonality represents, for the artist perhaps even more than for others, a great effort of will and understanding; he is generally unable to foresee clearly what his future development will be, and at the same time must believe with fanatical seriousness in what he is doing, even though he may have quite other preoccupations as soon as he has surmounted the problems in hand. "Do I contradict myself?" wrote Walt Whitman; "very well then, I contradict myself." The testimony of a composer has the authority and the vitality of intensely lived experience but his interpretations of that experience are constantly open to revision, even by myself. Too much weight, therefore should not be attached to his reported casual utterances, nor should too important conclusions be drawn from them.

●

Perhaps the most obvious symptom of the present crisis is its "confusion of tongues"—the result of nearly a century of musical development before the Great War. What took place during this period was a gradual dissociation of the musical consciousness of Europe (rather, of the Occident) into a multitude of various components. This dissociative process, the last phase of which constituted the "modern music" of twenty years ago, represented for the non-German peoples first of all a breaking-away from the German domination of musical culture, and was the inevitable result of the then latest developments of German music which, as Nietzsche once so penetratingly wrote, had ceased to be "the voice of Europe's soul" and was instead degenerating into mere *Vaterländerei*. Bach and Mozart, Beethoven and Schubert were German composers, to be sure, but not in any sense purely German in significance; Bruckner and Reger, even Strauss and Mahler—even, as Nietzsche points out, Schumann—in a far more restricted sense, were. The "voice of Europe's soul," however, has never yet been truly recovered; the *Vaterländerei* of which Nietzsche saw the fatal beginnings in Germany began to reproduce itself elsewhere in a franker and even more accentuated form, in a quantity of national "schools" of picturesquely local significance; the common cultural heritage began to be

**12**

abandoned in favor of localisms, until by the end of the century a very definite cleavage was perceptible.

The earlier years of our century brought definite signs of an even smaller division; a tendency towards an increasing number of purely individualistic and esoteric musical cults. Artists began to arise who no longer represented even a single land or a local culture, but rather isolated and even rootless yearnings of various kinds. "Prophets crying in the wilderness," unrecognized geniuses, the only defect of whose messages was their fatal subjectivity, appeared by the dozen; smaller spiritual stepsons of Wagner who, from an isolation essentially far deeper than that of Wagner, shouted their message to a fundamentally indifferent even though sometimes not wholly inattentive world, and who often strained and cracked their voices in the attempt to make themselves seriously heard. This was the age of "new possibilities," new technical devices, new and often quasi-religious esthetic creeds, symptoms of a fundamental insecurity and a lack of any but a purely passive inner necessity. The artist, taken by and large, was no longer fulfilling a

13

function as the voice of a real community of spirits; he had become rather a dealer in *articles de luxe* for a disabused aristocrary and a self-satisfied bourgeoisie. This type of music is well exemplified in the swollen and frenetically self-important works—not without a certain power—of a Scriabin; solitary orgies in which the once vital paroxysms of a Wagner are transported to a far thinner and more precious atmosphere. The more significant music of that time came to be representative of cities and of groups within cities, rather than of peoples. French music grew more and more essentially Parisian, German music to a certain extent polarized itself in Berlin and Vienna, even in Leipzig and Munich. But unlike the local Italian schools of painting in the Renaissance, these separate schools did not embody locally rooted expressions of a common human aspiration, but rather on the contrary, regional (often perhaps rather fortuitously regional) offshoots from a common background, a dissociative rather than a constructive movement. Many other factors contributed to this process; a constantly more complete rift between ''serious'' and popular music,

**14**

the growth of a type of virtuoso whose ideals are more those of the "prima donna" than of the genuinely interpretative artist—all of them, needless to say, factors by no means isolated, but part and parcel of the structure and the very essence of contemporary musical life.

•

The characteristic music of the post-war years has represented a complete contrast to the tendencies above described, and to some extent, in a very real sense, a reaction against them. That is not to say that the earlier types did not continue to exist, or even to deny the possibility of important figures among them. J. S. Bach is not the only historical example of an artist who in a sense outlived his time and yet who has loomed in the eyes of posterity far larger than any of his "modern" contemporaries. But the general movement since the war has been in a quite opposite direction. The composer who is most truly of today, whatever his nationality or esthetic creed, is no longer seeking "new possibilities" in the individualistic sense of the pre-war composers, but rather, in so far as he has a conscious program at all,

**15**

submitting himself to the new *necessities* of his time, and setting himself the new tasks which these necessities demand. The popular classification of "tendencies" of which mention has already been made has served to call attention to the fact of various differences of approach to these problems, even though it has not always thrown a very clear light on their deeper significance.

●

It is idle to inquire when and by whom the somewhat sweeping and inexact term "neo-classicism" was first applied to certain contemporary tendencies. It has been applied rather disconcertingly to such essentially different composers as Stravinsky, Hindemith, and Casella—composers in each of whom a certain more or less conscious traditionalism (not a new thing in art) is apparent, but who differ widely both in the traditions which they represent, and in the roles which tradition plays in the composition of their styles. There is also sometimes a still more primitive failure to discriminate between the traditionalism which springs from an essential impulse and is animated by a real inner tension, and another tra-

16

ditionalism, also to be found in recent music, which represents the exact contrary of this—a manner, a mode, nourished on *cliché* and fashionable propaganda—a traditionalism of followers and not of independent spirits. It is obviously not the latter that comes into consideration here.

Let us abandon, then, the term "neo-classicism" and consider rather certain features which this term is commonly taken to represent. Many of these features are not traditionalistic in any necessary sense, nor were they so in their origins. The composers in Russia and France who, during the latter half of the last century, made the original break with the specific latter-day German tradition, brought into the varied general current of music a mass of new and at first sometimes not wholly assimilated materials which were in contact with that tradition, or rather with those of its phases against which the break was directed. A more transparent texture, a pronounced emphasis on rhythm and movement, a less emphatic harmonic style, and an instrumentation consisting of sharply defined rather than mixed *timbres,* were char-

**17**

acteristic features of this newer music. What it lacked was first of all depth; it was very often music of association, of mood, of color, with relatively little essential and organic inner life of its own. Taken by and large it represented a collection of various *manners* rather than a style; an exploitation of certain nuances of color and sonority rather than a complete vision, a world in which all possible musical ingredients could find their place.

The true classical tradition of the seventeenth, eighteenth and early nineteenth centuries — the tradition which the Western world held in common under the leadership first of Italian and later of German musicians, was such a vision; and it was in a general sense to this tradition that musicians inevitably turned when they felt the need of a less limited and less external musical language and at the same time of that necessary connecting link with the past, without which art can never be more than a poor homunculus, essentially unnourished and incapable of organic growth.

This traditionalism, however, can in no real sense be called a "return to the past." Rather should it be considered in the light of a *reprise de contact;* and, in spite of its prophets, essentially nothing more than a point of departure. It was significant chiefly in that it marked the beginning of an instinctive effort to rediscover certain essential qualities of the older music with a view to applying them to the purposes of the new, an experiencing anew of certain laws which are inherent in the nature of music itself, but which had been lost from view in an increasing subjectivism and tendency to lean, even in "pure" music, more and more on association, sensation, and *Stimmung.*

This traditionalism, then, was essentially a part of a new attitude towards music—new at least for its time. Music began above all to be conceived in a more direct, more impersonal, and more positive fashion; there was a new emphasis on the dynamic, constructive, monumental elements of music, and, so to speak, a revaluation of musical materials. This revaluation has shown itself by no means only in actual compositions, but is perceptible among interpreters also. The function of the interpreter, in fact, has been to some extent reconsidered, and a far greater emphasis is today laid on fidelity to the composer's musical thought than was the case twenty years ago.

It would be inaccurate to define this current, as has been so often done, as an emphasis on "form" at the expense of "content;" it marks rather a change of attitude towards form and content both, which we might describe as a transference of the sphere of consciousness in the creative process. Whereas the earlier tendency was to be more and more conscious in regard to a "meaning behind the notes" and to construct the music according to principles derived from this indirect and not strictly musical source, the composers of the newer music proceeded directly from their musical impulses, seeking to embody these impulses in musical ideas which should have an independent existence of their own, and to develop these ideas according to the impetus inherent in them as musical entities. In other words, with the latter the *musical idea* is the point of departure, whereas with the former extra-musical considerations consciously determine the choice of the idea. The new attitude brought inevitably in its train a new and often laconic form of utterance which was sometimes interpreted as an abandonment of "expression." It was in reality, of course, a new manner of expression, a new sobriety and at its best, as in the finest pages of Stravinsky, a new inwardness. The grandiloquent and neurotic self-importance which characterized so much of the music of the years preceding the war has, in fact, practically disappeared and is only to be found in a few provincial survivals. The contemporary composer, when he wishes to achieve grandeur of utterance, does so by more subtle, monumental means.

It is assuredly false to conceive of music as having in any real sense moved away from "humanity." If it has in specific cases seemed to do so it is the result not of a false esthetic but of a defect of temperament in the composer. Music—pure music—has, naturally, everything to do with humanity, with the deepest human emotions and experiences. But the nature of this connection has sometimes been apprehended only in the vaguest manner; it is in any case not always so literal or so flat-footed a connection as certain literary gentlemen like to imagine. Images and associations are certainly often aroused by music, especially in those who are unaccustomed or insufficiently gifted musically to enter completely into an inner world where tones are sufficient. To say this is not to deny the value or even the interest of such experiences, but only to insist on their purely subjective nature. The inner experience of the thoroughbred musician who writes "program music" is, of course, an entirely contrary one, being in fact the instinctive translation of non-musical experience into tones, instead of a translation from tones into concrete conceptual terms. The very power of musical emotion lies precisely in the fact that it attaches itself *directly,* without any associational medium, to the most intimate experiences of the hearer; here lies also its universality, since, once a musical idiom is clearly grasped, it is accessible to everyone who lives and feels.

Needless to say, however, a new attitude towards what is technically called musical "form" does not necessarily mean that form in the truest sense has always been

**22**

achieved. Form in this sense is above all the full experience, to the point of complete fusion, of musical elements, and of the inner experiences behind them. It is present in a phrase, a rhythm, an instrumental trait, as surely as in a whole composition. In much contemporary music the inner experience is indeed there. The music is often *felt* and *heard,* by the composer; but how seldom is it felt and heard through to the limit! The experience behind it is too often explosive and spasmodic; it lacks the "great line" and the sharpness of contour which are the distinguishing—though not always immediately distinguishable—signs of a completely lived musical experience.

●

While by far the greater part of the more significant contemporary music composed outside of Central Europe, and very much of that composed in Germany as well, may be said to belong in a rough sense to the tendency above described, a large group of composers in the countries once included in the Austrian Empire, together with a perceptible number of Germans, have been following quite other lines. This so-called "Central European"

**23**

tendency is chiefly embodied in the works of Arnold Schönberg and his followers, though not strictly confined to them. Like the tendencies already described, it is an extremely complex phenomenon, composed of various contributing elements; while many of its features are of a strictly technical nature, too involved in their implications to be adequately discussed here. Nor must the qualification "Central European" be taken to imply an essentially local or geographical emphasis in the creed itself. Though in our belief it could, for historical reasons, have arisen nowhere else but in Vienna, and represents in fact an inevitable end-stage in Viennese musical culture, it claims for itself a universal validity, a more or less general monopoly, in fact, of what is significant in contemporary music. Far more than any other contemporary tendency it is dominated by a single personality, and its development is closely coincident with that of its leader.

A curious parallel with the beginnings of so-called "neo-classicism" may be seen in the definite formulation by Schönberg of the constructive principles of his school

—the well-known "twelve-tone system." The need for a fresh formal principle in contemporary music was felt, in other words, at very much the same moment by the leading spirits in the musical world and by composers of widely different feeling and background. The age of experiment was clearly over. New resources were at hand in profusion, many of them having been discovered by the very men who now felt the imperative need of absorbing them, organizing them, and wielding them into a new musical language.

The music of Schönberg and his pupils is still very inadequately known, even to musicians, and at least as much on account of its extreme material complexity as of its emotional content, it will probably for some time continue to be so. It is par excellence music for the "initiated" and it is difficult to see how it can ever reach a "great public."

The "twelve-tone system" has often been decried as a purely cerebral construction; and there is no question that some of its features are extremely dogmatic. It can not be too much stressed, however, that a system of this kind has no real existence apart from the works which embody it; it is the works of Schönberg and his followers that constitute what is vital in their contribution to contemporary music, not the system under which they are written.

It is necessary, then, to distinguish between Schönberg, Berg, and Webern, the composers, and Schönberg the musical theorist—perhaps again between these and Schönberg the teacher, in personal contact with his pupils. It is to the enormous credit of the latter that his pupils show a wide divergence of styles, and that their work—naturally in the cases of those who have real creative talent and background—bears witness to a profound artistic discipline.

It is hardly necessary to point out that the art of Schönberg has vital connections with the past. Close acquaintance shows how deeply it is rooted in the chromaticism of *Tristan* and *Parsifal*. This music may in fact be regarded as pre-eminently a logical development of that chromaticism, and the "twelve-tone system" as, in great part, a bold effort to formulate directive laws for its further development. "Atonality" if its real and not its superficial meaning be understood is merely another name for that chromaticism and not, as the term would seem to imply, a negation of the necessity for fundamental acoustic unity, based on laws which are the inevitable consequence both of natural phenomena of sound, and of the millenial culture of the Occidental ear. "Tonality" in the old, cadential sense, scarcely exists in any music of the present day, and where it can be said to exist in essence its nature has been so widened and modified as to render it unrecognizable to a composer of the last century. But the ultimate foundations on which the older tonal system was built, since they are inherent in the physical phenomena of resonance, remain unchanged; they can be enormously extended but scarcely modified.

All that is ambiguous and profoundly problematical in the music of Schönberg is to be traced to its definitely esoteric character. A contemporary German musician whose pronouncements in such matters are as authoritative as they are brilliant and profound, has compared certain musical tendencies in present day Germany to the decadent Greek art of Alexandria, remarking that, "There is an Alexandrianism of profundity and an Alexandrianism of superficiality." "Alexandrianism of profundity," indeed, well defines the music of the Central European group in certain respects — its tortured and feverish moods, its overwhelming emphasis on detail, its lack of genuine movement, all signs of a decaying musical culture, without fresh human impulses to keep it alive. The technic of this music, too, is of a curiously ambiguous nature, and often represents an extraordinary lack of coherence between the music *heard* and, so to speak, its theoretical structure — another sign of an art that is rapidly approaching exhaustion. An orchestral movement, for instance, which is constructed according to the most rigid contrapuntal mathematics will turn out to be, in its acoustic realization, a succession of interesting sonorities without audible contrapuntal implications—an impression not to be dispelled by the most conscientious and sympathetic study of the score, the most complete familiarity with both its intellectual and its sonorous content. An opera whose remarkable feature when heard is

**28**

its fidelity to the text, its responsiveness to every changing psychological nuance, proves on examination to be constructed in its various scenes on the external models of classic forms, without, however, the steady and consistent movement that gives these forms their purpose and their character. Such esoteric and discarded devices as the *cancrizans* variation of a theme, a technical curiosity which is admittedly inaccessible to the most attentive ear and which was used with the utmost rarity by the classic composers, becomes a regular and essential technical procedure. All of this goes to indicate the presence of a merely speculative element, tending to be completely dissociated from the impression actually received by the ear and the other faculties which contribute to the direct reception of a musical impression, and to produce what is either a fundamentally inessential *jeu d'esprit* of sometimes amazing proportions, or a kind of scaffolding erected as an external substitute for a living and breathing musical line.

Such reflections, however, are necessarily but approximative and by no means dispose of this music and the problems which it raises. A work of art is a positive reality and must be so considered, quite apart from the principles which are to be found within it. Thus one may reject many of Schönberg's ideas and modes of procedure while acknowledging not only his historical position as the initiator of even more in contemporary music than is usually accredited to him, but also his work, and that of some of his followers, as in itself an important and fundamentally unassailable element in the music of this time.

●

Less strictly musical in significance than either of the general currents discussed above, but highly characteristic of our time and therefore worthy of some discussion, is the deliberate movement on the part of musicians, especially in Germany but also to a certain extent elsewhere, to seek a new relationship with the public and to form a great variety of new and direct contacts with it. The past ten years have witnessed the production of a vast quantity of music definitely written for purposes of practical "consumption," and though many of those purposes do not offer a precisely new field for musical pro-

**30**

duction, new, on the other hand, is the scale and extent of the interest which musicians are taking in them.

As has been pointed out, the movement is to a large extent economic in character, and the necessities to which it responds are outer rather than inner necessities; but in several respects it is symptomatic and must command the attention of everyone who is interested in the way music may go in the future. For it represents a direct attempt to meet the crisis not only in its material but in several of its spiritual aspects as well.

The movement is therefore only in a partial sense an artistic one. It originated no doubt during the economic chaos in Germany just after the war, in the period of "inflation," when the economic breakdown of the German bourgeoisie led to a profound modification of the musical life of Germany, partly by reducing considerably the public able to attend concerts and operatic performances, and partly by taking the attention of the new generation away from cultural interests—a situation later made more acute by the political, intellectual, and moral unrest which followed. It was under the pressure of such realities that many musicians were forced to take stock of the whole place of music in present-day society and to seek new channels for their activity. They found these new channels in the constructive movements of the time, to which they sought to contribute the energies which music could give. Emphasis was laid above all on the practical purposes of the music thus produced; music was above all to cease to be an article of luxury or a primarily individual self-expression; to serve rather the ends of education, and especially of political and social propaganda. The same idea, far more drastically applied, will be readily recognized as that underlying the attitude of Soviet Russia towards art.

On perhaps a higher plane, the movement was undoubtedly in part the beginning of a renewed search for a fresh and more actively participating public. Composers busied themselves with the formation of a genuinely popular style, with rendering their music more accessible through a simplification of technic, with applying themselves seriously to the new problems offered by the radio, the cinema and mechanical means of reproduction. New ideals began to appear in the opera; younger composers began to produce works designed definitely for momentary consumption, works which were above all striking and "actual," designed to fulfill a momentary purpose and to be scrapped as soon as that purpose was fulfilled. They recognized, as did Wagner in a wholly different sense before them, the importance and the possibilities of opera in the creation of a public capable of the kind of participation which truly binds the composer to his world and his time.

The movement deserves close attention, as has already been said, not for its inherent artistic importance, but rather because of the questions it raises. Various ones among its enthusiastic promoters have deserted the ranks, and the movement itself seems to have settled down to its place as a more or less subordinate element in the musical activity of Germany. It nevertheless still exerts a strong influence, especially in the direction of opera, where it has undoubtedly influenced the character and quality of new productions by enlisting the services of the *avant-garde* of modern stage production.

Its chief interest, however, lies in the fact that by the very act of facing them, it has drawn attention to certain modern problems and dilemmas which may at any time become acute in other countries than Germany. A continuance and deepening of the present economic crisis cannot help but bring profound changes in the cultural life of every country; the universally reactionary movement in the musical life of the present season might easily be a mere foretaste of a greater tendency towards apathy and stagnation—a tendency which would be far more serious in any other country than in Germany with her incomparably more highly organized and ubiquitous musical activity. The composer will then be forced to conquer an entirely different public, potential or actual, than the one which is now prepared sooner or later to understand him. Under the circumstances the least that he can do is to examine carefully the moving principles of his relation to his art, and the relation of his art to the world, and to face both with a seriousness worthy of the occasion.

●

There is talk, nowaday, of a "return to expression"—

talk the vagueness of which is slightly discouraging, it never being made quite clear what kind of expression is meant. Furthermore a certain crudity of understanding is evident in the implication that expression in any essential sense has been forsworn.

No doubt it was necessary—intimately and imperatively necessary—at a given moment for composers to rid their systems of certain poisons: of a rhetoric which had lost its vitality and degenerated into mere attitudinizing. No doubt it was necessary for them to become once more aware of music in its direct and sensuous aspects, to re-experience the simplest musical facts, in and for themselves, with a new freshness of sensation and perception. No doubt, too, this necessity no longer exists; many composers have gained through the experiences of the past ten years a fresh suppleness of style and of movement, a fresh sense of musical values, which they are able to apply with constantly greater freedom. The currents above described are all to a large extent characterized by a certain tenseness and lack of free movement which is inseparable at first from any far-reaching spiritual revolu-

**35**

tion or readjustment. But nothing could be farther from the truth than the idea that any art worthy of the name can be self-consciously guided in one direction or another, or that it consists in a series of short term "movements," "tendencies," and the like. Viewed in perspective the past fifteen years will appear as short and at least as inconclusive as any other fifteen years, and its fruits will be judged not by the fluctuation of the present fashions, but by living accomplishments, many and possibly even the most characteristic of which cannot yet have had time to become mature or in any sense definitive.

Thus far, then, a "return to expression" or any other new "tendency" has yet to become clearly defined—that is, it has not as yet incorporated itself in a vigorous new personality which shows clear and striking signs of having surmounted the inner conflicts necessary to fruition, and of having begun the apparently equally inevitable outer conflicts and struggles for recognition which every freshly authentic personality must face. This is not at all to say that no such personality will arise. There are still interesting and fresh beginnings from which much can be hoped and expected, and it must be remembered that a tortured and restless period like these post-war years—unquestionably, and for America as well as Europe the severest trial through which Western civilization has passed—is not one which favors the easy emergence of really commanding personalities, in art any more than in other fields. Yet it is obviously only through the emergence of such personalities that collapse can be avoided, or the crisis, even in its purely temporary aspects, be resolved. When it ceases to be a spiritual and moral crisis, it will cease to be in any but a very momentary sense a material one.

●

The above reflections are not precisely encouraging, perhaps; but the facts behind them are rather inescapable. To ignore these facts is to ignore fundamental realities of the present-day musical world, a sign of weakness or provincialism, and of a fundamental lack of contact with life. Awareness of them in some aspect or other is indeed the one common ground possible to contemporary composers. The various currents briefly sketched above have represented efforts, dictated by instinctive necessity, to meet these facts with positive achievements—perhaps they may eventually prove to be preliminary contributions to something like a common effort.

In the opinion of the writer of these reflections, such efforts have hitherto been incomplete, because based on an insufficiently profound and daring spiritual experience. It would seem to be obvious that a real community of spirits cannot be created in the realm of music alone, nor can it arise in music without a simultaneous or even previous stirring towards a new human solidarity.

Art is of course governed by necessities; it goes the way it must go. The artist needs all his faculties, then, in becoming constantly more fully aware of these necessities; of listening attentively to their stirrings in himself, and meeting them with all of the forces as his disposal. He cannot make even the smallest vital contribution to the art which he serves unless he has the courage to remain unceasingly aware of the fundamental impulses within himself, and, from his own unshakable point of vantage, to participate freely in the vital impulses of the world of which he is a part. He must discipline himself to be content only with realities, in the deepest sense, since only on realities can a true culture, a true basis for human development and felicity, be built.

It may well be that the energies of the present day will, for some time to come, prove capable only of achievements of an intrinsically incomplete nature. But an age of confusion may be also an age of the greatest hope, and discussions as to the ultimate specific value of contemporary art are irrelevant and in the deepest sense amateurish. The truly mature artist does not ask himself such questions, since he knows that a life lived in an uncompromisingly creative spirit, or even the creation of a single genuine bar or phrase is a more exhilarating and essential experience than an infinite amount of ''success,'' contemporary or posthumous. It is, however, hardly a matter of choice; in the absence of vital inner necessities, worthy the attention of a fully adult human being, music, or any other form of art, is scarcely worth bothering about.

[1933]

**39**

# BORIS DE SCHLOEZER

"To understand music..." — this is an expression which all of us, professionals and laymen alike, use constantly, for the most part without considering its precise meaning; without really knowing, even, whether this term "to understand" is applicable to music, whether we can say: "I do not understand Stravinsky," as we say ordinarily: "I do not understand English," or "I do not understand Kant." What difference is there between a musical work which we understand and another which we do not? Is there, in a word, anything which can be understood in a musical work? To understand is an intellectual operation: does music appeal to the intellect? And if we say that it does, if we suppose that the intellect plays a part in hearing music, must we conclude that it determines the pleasure and the emotion which a musical composition affords? Or does comprehension follow rather upon the heels of emotion?

These are questions whose complexity and difficulty are

increased by the lack of a precise terminology. When we speak of art and, in particular, of music, we feel that we can dispense with words sharply defined; we even prefer, it seems, to remain in penumbral obscurity. For is not music essentially vague, non-precise, forever in flux? How should we seize it by means of rigid concepts, rigidly articulated?

The term "to understand" can only be applied to music if music possesses some meaning. To understand any proposition whatever is to grasp its significance, to apprehend what it *means,* its objective value symbolized by the words which compose this proposition and the relations between these words. Those who hear a speech can react in different, often contradictory ways to the words of the speaker. From this point of view there is a complete analogy between a mass-meeting, for example, and a concert. Like the playing of the virtuoso, the words of the speaker are the product of certain intellectual and emotional conditions transformed to a series of sonorous vibrations which in turn provoke physiological and psychological reactions in the audience. But in the case of the speaker the reactions are evidently conditioned, in part at least, by the content of his speech, by the meaning of his words. They have a certain objective value of which the words are only symbols and which the audience must understand. If the speaker is urging war and part of his audience understand him to be pleading for peace, we say quite simply that they are mistaken, that they have misunderstood the speaker. Language, written or spoken, possesses a content independent of the individual reactions it arouses.

Now is this also true of musical language? Or does what happens in a concert hall reduce itself finally to the psychological condition of the player, to the sound vibrations, and to the multiple psychological reactions in the audience?

It is certain that a melody, a rondo, a sonata are stripped of all rational content; we do not put ideas and theories into music. Theories and ideas may give birth to musical works: but between these works and the psychological, emotional and intellectual soil from which they spring there is absolutely nothing in common. Language is a system of signs which we decipher to get at their meaning, and the whole value of words rests for us in this meaning. But when, on the other hand, we try to decipher the meaning of a piece of music, when we attempt to treat it is as a system of signs, to pass through it to something else, we cease to listen to music: we have let the sounds escape and have found nothing in their place. In music the sound system is perceived as such, it possesses for us a certain intrinsic value. It can indeed produce violent emotions and initiate multiple associations, but nevertheless it is as a sonorous system that it persists in consciousness and is enjoyed.

This drives us to the following alternative: either music means nothing, possesses no objective content, and resolves itself entirely into sonorous vibrations that are essentially ephemeral and emotional states: or else the relationship between what we shall call briefly content and form in music is wholly different from any relationship which exists in ordinary language.

## II

What, then, is the relationship in ordinary language?

**44**

It is one of *transcendence*. The ideas of discourse, the content, the sense of a sentence transcend its form, its sonorous body. To understand spoken or written language is precisely to pass beyond it to get at something else. Insofar as words are only signs, what they mean is something other than themselves. That is why one can summarize a speech or a conversation, extract the ideas and the meaning. Now it is absolutely impossible to summarize a musical work, to extract anything whatsoever from it. If we attempt to epitomize a sonata we simply get another sonata built on the same themes.

It would be a grave error to consider the themes of a symphony, for example, as its content, and to establish in this way an analogy between the development through which a writer guides his ideas and the development which a composer imposes upon his themes. The two fundamental themes of a sonata allegro in no sense "summarize" this sonata; they are not at all ideas in the sense in which we say, for example, that class warfare is the fundamental idea in the speeches of this or that socialist leader. If the musical work possesses a certain content, a significance, if it means something, its meaning is inherent in the work itself and is equally present in the whole and in each of its parts. The content here cannot be external to what we call form: it is *immanent* in this form.

But does this relation of immanence belong exclusively to music?—do we find it also in the other arts? Thus far I have employed a parallel between music and "common language" which is solely a means of communication and quite without esthetic value. But if we penetrate the realm of literature and poetry, we find that the relation of transcendence which binds content and form in ordinary language is superseded by a relation of immanence. The word is no longer merely a sign which we decipher to get at something else that it symbolizes, but now possesses intrinsic value. Although it is easy enough to summarize the average magazine article, summary is not so easy if we have before us a page from some great writer, for his ideas fuse as it were with the words which express them —they are imbedded in, or, rather, embodied in, those words. One may, indeed, give the gist of a funeral oration by Bossuet, but this extract no longer has anything in common with the work of Bossuet. The fusion of sense and form is even more integral in verse. Thus it is as impossible to summarize a sonnet by Baudelaire as a rondo by Mozart. Here we are on the border-line of music, which is the ideal limit (in the mathematical sense of the term) of poetry. Poetry tends towards music insofar as it aspires to immanence, and fails to become music insofar as the words still retain a certain transcendent significance, insofar as we still recognize them as signs.

From this point of view, all artistic activity tends to *transform into immanent values signs having only transcendent significance.* Music is thus the purest of the arts, since it retains nothing whatsoever that is a sign or representation of some other reality outside itself.

### III

When I read a text, any text whatever, I can interpret it and comment on it in any number of ways but it is impossible for me to extract anything other than its meaning, if it has a precise meaning at all. I read, for example, in the obituary column of a newspaper, that Mr. X has just died after a long illness; unless I read hastily and inaccurately I cannot possibly deduce from this text that Mr. X died suddenly. One conception alone is correct, all others false; since language possesses a transcendent content, this content can be extracted, analyzed, and made to serve as a check upon all other readings. The meaning of a musical phrase (admitting that such a thing exists) is on the contrary immanent in this phrase: it cannot therefore be checked, it cannot be detached and formulated in rational terms.

If we ask a pianist who has just played a ballad by Chopin what it means, the only thing he can do is to play the same ballad over again. But it would be incorrect to conclude that music "means nothing" or that its content is vague. Untranslatable though it may be, the musical sense of the work can be extremely precise, as exact as that of a scientific work. And when I say "musical sense" I am not thinking merely of the emotional repercussions in the audience, repercussions varying to infinity, but of a certain spiritual content which belongs only to this

**48**

work, which constitutes at once its essence and its form, its concrete reality, its individuality.

Nevertheless the question posed at the beginning still persists. The term "to understand" can be applied to music only if music possesses a definite spiritual content, and this content, if it exists, can only be immanent in the work. But does it exist?

It is impossible to offer a direct proof of this existence, since what this or that work signifies cannot be formulated rationally. But I shall try to show that if we deny all objective significance to the sonorous work we are driven finally to subjective conceptions that destroy music.

Either the musical work (a sonata by Beethoven, for example) possesses an objective significance, contains a definite spiritual message, like a poem, a novel, or else its text is immaterial only, and there are as many sonatas, opus 101, as there are pianists; or rather, since most pianists do not always play in the same way, as many as there are executions of the work throughout the world. But we must go still further: the execution of the sonata at the concert evidently provokes varied and contradictory reactions among the audience. These reactions, whatever they may be, whoever the auditors may be, are all equally valid. By what standard shall we judge them? What then is a musical work if denied objective significance? A system of sonorous vibrations on the one hand, and, on the other, individual emotions; and, therefore, to go one step further it is a set of black marks on paper, traced by the hand of the composer, which the player deciphers with the help of certain conventions, and which serve to construct sound waves the hearing of which evokes multiple physiological and psychological reactions. The composer of opus 101 is no more, the thoughts, the desires, the images of which the work is the product have vanished. There remain only these marks on paper, a sort of scheme for the player, who is perfectly free to do as he wishes. One will draw out sublimity, another what is merely amusing, a third the grotesque. The player who happens to make us laugh with the sonata, opus 101, will thus be just as right as the other who moves us to tears; only the interpreter who bores us will be wrong. Finally, we can no longer restrict the question to the sonata proper; what is true of it is also true of the interpretation by this or that pianist, on this or that day, in this or that concert hall. There remain then only the thousand varied images in the consciousness of thousands of auditors, images sublime, grotesque, farcical, dull. This is the logical consequence of the subjectivism in vogue with so many people who do not usually think matters through to the end but content themselves with a moderate and comfortable scepticism.

## IV

There is still another aspect of the question which it is impossible to neglect. If we consider only the power which music so eminently has to evoke intense reactions among its auditors, and to create among them in this way, for a few moments, a sort of collective soul, a relation then emerges between music and various other stimuli which men have always widely employed. Between the influence of music and that of alcohol, of hashish, etc., we no longer find any qualitative distinction.

Thus today we gather people about a piano and act upon them by means of sound waves; and tomorrow, perhaps, we shall get still better results by means of an electric current acting directly upon the skin. What is important is the result, is it not? All that matters is *what happens* when people are subjected to the influence of these waves, these rays, these emanations.

If music is only the art of combining sounds in a manner agreeable to the ear, in a fashion which gives birth in us to a variety of emotions, I really do not see in what way the art of the perfumer, or of the cook, is inferior. In this case we shall have to admit the possibility of those "symphonies of odors" or of gustatory sensations which the hero of *A Rebours* tried to construct, and shall have to grant them an esthetic value of the same order as that of musical symphonies. A dish, a perfume are as able as a melody to call forth reactions of feeling, images, ideas. There is no reason to stop here: tactile sensations, odors, tastes, can stir up tempests in the soul and produce ecstasies in comparison with which the pleasures of music seem pale indeed.

**52**

And what is one to do about expression? Has not music a certain power to be found neither in a "symphony of odors" nor in a dinner?

Music is, of course, eminently expressive. The musical work is always the outcome of certain mental attitudes in the artist, conscious or unconscious, whether he wishes it or not; it always carries the mark of his personality, the burden of his feeling, of his hopes, of his spiritual experience. The need for self-realization, for self-expression, certainly plays a very great role in the desire that imperiously drives a musician to creation; and if the labor of creation holds a certain joy, it arises, in part at least, from a very clear feeling of deliverance. But this expressive character which the composer finds in music, depends precisely upon the fact that the musical work possesses a definite content. If the work had no spiritual reality (objective in relation to the emotions of the auditors), if it could be reduced to the numberless mental attitudes which it evokes, it would have by the same token no expressive power.

Now this *is* the case with combinations of olfactory,

tactile and gustatory impressions: they are a means of excitation; one may, by using them cleverly, arouse the most diverse emotions; but they have no expressive value. In other words, they offer to the artist no possibility of realizing his personality, of externalizing and of liberating himself. The reason is that they have no intellectual content—"signify" nothing, mean nothing. Art, on the contrary, exists only where there is intellectuality.

If the musical work is not a direct appeal addressed to our intelligence (I take this term for the moment in its broadest sense), if it possesses no objective significance, it can find no place in the domain of art and is indistinguishable from a lover's caress or a cream-puff. This expressive power itself, which we all agree to concede to music, is only the consequence, the secondary effect of the act by which we grasp what it means. We are thus led to the conclusion that the music does possess a spiritual content immanent in the work, which it concerns us to understand.

Still, even those who recognize that a page of music has significance, means something, are apt to regard it not

**54**

as specific but general and vague, and thus they explain the powerful evocative action of this art, in which each one ultimately finds what he looks for, what he himself contributes, colored by idiosyncrasies of mind, temperament and desire. Metaphysical theories of music — Schopenhauer's among others — consider the matter always, if I am not mistaken, from this point of view: they seek to confer upon the art of sounds a certain spiritual value, a significant content, but hold that this content can only be general and not precise. I myself have upon occasion (speaking of the *Octuor* of Stravinsky) said that music contains no specific idea, not because it contains nothing but because it contains everything.

Now it seems to me that we are on the wrong track here, and that our error is linked with that other fundamental one of confusing the repercussions of music in us—our individual and variable reactions when confronted by a melody—with its significance, its spiritual content. I turn again to the example of the obituary notice in a newspaper. It is read by thousands. Their reactions are evidently very different, varying with the degrée of acquaintance with the man now dead. The announcement of this death will be differently colored for each, will carry a burden of varying images and associations. And yet the content of this announcement is *one,* and all the emotions which it can arouse are conditioned by an act of intellection. In the case of the musical work, the content cannot be extracted from the form, the very body of the work; for content in music, as we have pointed out, is immanent in the form.

Everything that floats about a page of music is vague and indefinite; but if it is impossible for us to define, this is not because its significance is too vague and general; on the contrary, it is because it is *too concrete.* Describing a prelude by Chopin we meet the same difficulty which confronts us when we attempt to define an individual being. The meaning of this prelude is its very aspect. We are dealing with something absolutely unique, and this is the explanation of our impotence in the presence of a musical work, impotence analogous to that which we feel when we seek by formulas, howsoever flexible and subtle, to represent a living being: this Jean, this Pierre, whose very name is a general symbol which does not cover this *hic et nunc*. Only direct contact, intuition itself, can unveil the living being. The musical work also must be seized directly. If the content of music would admit of generalization, a knowledge of it would for that very reason be easy, no matter how fluid and indefinite this content might be.

In the arts where form can to some extent be distinguished from the content (the plastic and poetic), such knowledge is possible, even though it always remains approximate, since the soul of every artistic production is after all fused with its body, as our bodies and souls are fused. The art of sounds alone succeeds in achieving an *absolute* fusion and in creating values. ideas which are concrete beings, personalities whose essence is, so to speak, one with their appearance. From this point of view, therefore, music is the least "modest" of all the arts; she offers herself to us altogether, for she has nothing to hide—her most cherished secret is precisely her surface.

## V

Thus it must be admitted that every musical work possesses a certain spiritual content, definite and concrete, immanent, consequently impossible to formulate in rational terms. The emotional influence of the work, its expressive power, depends upon the act by which we grasp its objective content: to be moved by music we must first understand what it means. A reading of Spinoza's *Ethics* can arouse profound emotions in us, but they represent only our individual reactions to the ideas of the treatise, ideas which we must first of all understand, and which are independent of our mental attitudes. The only difference between the work of Spinoza and the sonata, opus 101, is that we can examine the content of the *Ethics* apart from the form, while in the case of Beethoven or of any other musician this operation is forbidden. We are thus led to the conclusion that "musical comprehension" presents certain peculiarities; music is not a symbol like written or spoken language, but is the very thing itself which it is necessary to understand.

Before analyzing further the sense of the term "to

**58**

understand'' as applied to music, I should like for a moment to consider the sensuous pleasure which music affords, for a good many people regard this as the primordial element of the art, completely independent of intellectual processes. Indeed to many acute minds it seems possible to enjoy music physically, without at all understanding it.

The question then is whether this pleasure is essential, whether it is inherent in all musical perception; in a word whether we are dealing here with a primary or secondary element. Even if it should be established that the hearing of a work is unfailingly accompanied by physical pleasure, it might still be true that this pleasure is caused by something else.

It is necessary, moreover, to rigorously distinguish this sensuous pleasure from the joy, *sui generis,* which every work of art affords, and which contains, esthetically transmuted, the negative, enervating emotions that in real life we seek to avoid: melancholy, despair, etc. This joy has an intellectual aspect and differs in kind from relatively simple sensuous pleasure.

**59**

I say "some," because it would be inaccurate to assume—and this answers the first question posed above—that physical pleasure, sonorous delight, is essential to the hearing of music. At different epochs, with different composers, it has played a role more or less important; but it is impossible to see here the *sine qua non* of esthetic emotion, any more than for the other arts. Certain composers offer us this pleasure of the senses, but the productions of others are cold and austere and seem to tend towards an ascetic art from which all physical voluptuousness would be banished. In the number of the *voluptueux* one might place Mozart, Couperin and most of the clavecinists, Rossini and the Italian masters; among the romantics, Chopin particularly; closer to ourselves, Debussy and Ravel; among the young men, Poulenc.

But here we are in the domain of personal taste, of subjective impressions and judgments which allow of no discussion: this or that composer whose sonorities ravish our ears will seem to others dry, hard and painful. And the very composer who offered us only severe, intellectual joys seems suddenly a sensual enchanter, and vice versa. It is certain that we appreciate Debussy in quite another fashion than did his first admirers. Wagner cannot on the whole be classed among the "hedonists;" and yet certain episodes of the *Tetralogy* or of *Tristan* afford the ear a genuinely physical pleasure. This pleasure, on the other hand, we now feel but rarely on listening to the music of Beethoven, though in the past it was otherwise. In a word, the sonorous delight which certain composers dispense so generously and others seem on principle to avoid (without always succeeding), is an unstable and capricious thing. In any case it would be as ridiculous to banish it from music on the pretext that it degrades (the sensuous charm of a *Nocturne* by Chopin or of a *Prelude* by Debussy does not at all weaken the spiritual significance of these passages) as it would be to insist that it be always present, denying all esthetic value to works which are not ingratiating.

Musical emotion then, can develop in the absence of all sensuous pleasure, and even when the first hearing is painful. But is even this pleasure an immediate sensation, pure of all intellectual alloy? Is it of the same order as the pleasure a well prepared dish affords us?

Experience and reason alike show us that the pleasures of sound are but faintly analogous with the pleasures of taste, of touch or of smell, since they involve a comprehension of the work from which they derive. In order that music afford us a sensuous physical pleasure, we must first have understood it. This pleasure, supposedly simple and direct, is the result of the intellectual grasp of a sequence; to delight in a succession of sounds, a melody, as we delight in a well cooked dish, we must apprehend the relations between these sounds. The physical charm of a Debussy, for example, can be felt only when one begins to find one's bearings in his music; and there undoubtedly are still people for whom the *Cathedrale Engloutie* is nothing but a chaotic medley of chords, who will never find in it any delight. If some sonorous combination happens to tickle their ears agreeably, the next chord, for them unrelated to the preceding, will immediately shatter the charm. For the person who understands, on the contrary, the pleasure is born precisely of this passing from one sonority to another, each acquiring its whole value only in relation with those which precede and follow. The pleasure an uncomprehending auditor may happen to find in one or another of these chords does not differ essentially from the pleasure afforded us sometimes by the vibration of a telegraph wire, the murmur of a brook, etc. It is not a specifically musical, esthetic pleasure; it is merely one of the more or less agreeable sensations which our environment often offers, sensations that awaken vague images, fugitive emotions, and conspire to keep us in a certain state of well-being but which have nothing at all to do with art.

## VI

If I dwell so insistently upon the distinction to be made between the complex reactions of those who hear a musical work and the act by which they grasp the meaning immanent in its sonorous body, this is because the attention of critics and estheticians is ordinarily concentrated upon these individual reactions in an effort to determine the laws which govern them. These laws exist, perhaps; for the constant physiological and psychological action of certain intervals and certain timbres seems indubit-able. We are familiar with the theories so widespread today, which hold the musical work to be an ensemble of dynamic schemes acting upon us according to a definite rhythm: tension-resolution. There is certainly truth in these theories, but it cannot be too often repeated that psycho-physiological experiments and considerations neglect exactly those esthetic facts which most need ex-planation; the specific element which distinguishes our reactions to a musical work from those which the flux of real life provides.

For the rest, we must recognize that a large portion of a concert audience, a much larger one even than we think, does not listen to the music, does not even know what it means to listen to music: for them music is merely a stim-ulant which plunges them into vague reveries to which they abandon themselves more or less unconsciously. It would greatly surprise impassioned "amateurs" to be told that to listen to a work is to be active, to accom-plish a task sometimes actually painful, demanding a certain preparation, and that their exclusively passive attitude towards the sonorous text prevents them not only from grasping its meaning, but also from enjoying the specific pleasure it might have imparted had they followed attentively, instead of giving themselves up, like opium smokers, to the play of their imaginations.

It would be false, nevertheless, to conclude from this that the comprehension of music necessarily demands a knowledge of musical technic and that it is impossible to appreciate a musical work, to grasp its meaning, without possessing the elements of what one might call the musical grammar. There is an ambiguity here, it seems to me, which it is absolutely essential to dissipate. To understand a page of music — a sonata by Beethoven, a rondo by Mozart, a fugue by Bach—is not the same thing as to be able to make a technical analysis of these pages. One may understand form, harmony and counterpoint and still remain deaf to the work of which every element is perceived and named. I do not say that a knowledge of musical technic does not aid in comprehension; but we do have two absolutely different operations here.

The history of music and of musical criticism proves

this to us conclusively. It is needless, I suppose, to cite examples of the total lack of comprehension often exhibited by the most learned theoreticians when confronted by musical productions which they were nevertheless perfectly capable of analyzing step by step. And we may remember on the other hand the discoveries made in music by men wholly without technical knowledge: it was not the conservatory professors who discovered Wagner, Debussy and Stravinsky for us. One may be an excellent grammarian, and still be at a loss before a sentence of this or that obscure writer—even though one can perfectly well point out the subject, the verb, the complement. But in ordinary language the words and their relations have a symbolic character; there is nothing surprising then in the fact that grammatical analysis is sometimes insufficient to give us immediately the logical significance of a sentence: if the meaning of but one sign escapes us the sentence no longer has any sense for us, no matter how clear it may be syntactically. Now since it is conceded that a musical work is not a sign, it is then pertinent to ask why its structure does not give

**66**

us its meaning directly, and why, moreover, its meaning is often revealed to those incapable of analyzing the work formally.

This difficulty is superficial only; it is obviated as soon as we examine the problem closely. To understand a melody, a phrase, a musical work, is to perceive its unity; in other words, we understand a series of sounds when we succeed in making of this series a system, a coherent whole. And it is in this whole alone that each of the moments of the sonorous flow which we follow so attentively acquires its full value and its reality. The difference between the man who understands music and the man who does not, is simply this: the first perceives a system of complex relations, the second perceives only isolated sounds. For him who comprehends, an isolated sound is only an abstraction; the reality is the system which integrates these sounds.

An organism is not a mere composite of two arms, two legs, a torso, etc.; these very members exist only in an individual whole and as functions of this whole. In the same way the slightest melody is not a mere composite of sounds disposed in a certain order, according to a certain rhythm, but is an entity of a particular sort, unique, inimitable, lending its essential character to each of the elements which analysis reveals. Just as the word *luxe* in the celebrated verse of Baudelaire possesses unique sonority and a significance absolutely different from what it might have in a fashion report, so the sound which we call *do* changes altogether in passing from one musical composition to another; we may say, in brief, that we are never dealing with the same sounds and that there are as many *do's* and *re's* etc., as there are musical organisms.

This sonorous flood which vanishes as soon as it is born we grasp, in so far as we understand it, as a certain stable, definite and objective reality. But this reality does not transcend the sound: it is what constitutes their immanent unity, what gives them a precise significance. We see now why analyzing a musical work is not the same thing as understanding it. Technical analysis gives us at best only the abstract formula of a work, and thus reduces it to a certain type; while to understand a piece of music is to recreate its unique personality as it first emerged in the mind of the composer.

This recreation does not require a memory capable of retaining the whole of the work from beginning to end, something very few can do. The synthesis proceeds progressively, moving with the flood of sound, each moment of which thus bears, in a sense, the accumulated burden of the preceding moments—not because we *remember* them, but because we perceive each of them as direct functions of those which have preceded. Having come to the end of the piece, we have perhaps forgotten the beginning and might in any case be unable to reconstruct it, but the work well understood is found again and exists integrally in the concluding chord: a person entering the hall at this moment would hear merely a simple perfect chord, but for the rest of us who have integrated it in a definite system it possesses a specific sonorous value.

If we regard the matter from this point of view, the diversity of reactions among an audience in the presence of a musical work and the varying avatars into which different interpreters shape this music at various times does not at all affect its integrity: what makes an organism of it, what constitutes its formal unity, exists always. *In so far as they have grasped this unity, in so far as they have perceived the work as a complex whole, the auditors,* whatever may be their secondary reactions, *will understand it in the same way; it will reveal the same thing to them, namely, what it is.* Only the secondary reactions change. It is certain that today, before a *Passion* by Bach, for example, we have other emotions, other thoughts that had the contemporaries of Bach and the composer himself; but there is only one way of understanding it.

[1930]

**70**

INK DRAWING BY CARLOS DYER

INK DRAWING BY CARLOS DYER

# ADOLPH WEISS

The twelve-tone series is a definite arrangement of all tones of the chromatic scale in a set order. It is applied in all the forms of variation, harmonically or contrapuntally, horizontally or vertically, to the construction of every detail of a twelve-tone composition. The twelve-tone series is the "law" of the composition, the working material, not the theme but only the material for the theme. Any tone of the series may be used in any octave position, according to the discrimination of the composer. Tone relations are not binding in the sense of direction or position. The series may be divided or sub-divided into smaller groups of related motives, and any group may be joined to any other to form new combinations. "Free" tones (those that do not belong in the strict sequence of the series) may be interpolated between tones of the series, or between the groups composing it. The twelve-tone series may be used in transposition and in all sorts of combinations. Often the tones are scattered

**75**

among various voices. Sometimes they are only the first notes of a sequential figuration. Naturally the various methods of applying the series will not always be immediately perceptible to the ear.

It is an outgrowth of the esthetic and logical implications of the chromatic system, which has the chromatic scale as its foundation, in contradistinction to the diatonic, which uses major, minor and other modes. Its possibilities are unlimited, first because the choice of the series (which takes the place of the key, scale, or tonality) is arbitrary; second, because chordal construction is not restricted to building up by thirds, fourths, or fifths, etc.; and third, because the greatest "freedom" in coordination is left to the taste and discretion of the composer.

Members of the Schönberg school differ widely in their individual application of this technic. Such individuality is ensured by the plasticity of the system. There are those who cannot yet discern great differences in the works of the Schönbergians, to whom "in the dark all cats are black." But let them observe the rhythmic construction and the spiritual content if the fine differences in harmonic construction are not apparent. Remember that Beethoven, Mozart, Haydn and others used practically the same harmonic formulæ, those of the diatonic system.

[1932]

**77**

# ERNST KRENEK

There is a hardly a composer—and the whole of musical history cannot show us a similar example—whose major works are played so rarely, relatively speaking, and are so utterly unknown in their tonal form, as those of Arnold Schönberg. Nor is there another composer who, when all is said and done, has brought to bear upon the generation of his contemporaries such far-reaching and compelling influences. There is no living musician who, having once had an electrifying contact with Schönberg's creations, has not received from this contact some sort of definite direction. Those who deny this fact usually betray themselves by the intensity of their denial.

The figure of Schönberg is surrounded by an atmosphere of salon scandal, provoked by genuine vexation; the existence of this figure alone exercises a singular influence on the musical development of the present era. Sooner or later everyone is forced to a climactic inner decision. The manner in which a person reveals himself at this critical point is usually of marked importance to his artistic future. Those who cannot meet Schönberg's challenge try to dismiss him as an heretical monomaniac, and they aim their criticism at the sectarian fanaticism and spineless devotion of his disciples. It is neither necessary nor possible to refute such accusations—for of all these aspects, the one conspicuous fact is his status as prophet. With such figures as Schönberg the important thing is not their capacity for tolerance, but solely their mental power for argument.

Wherein now consist the singular historical values of his achievement which alone can justify such an attitude? That he created "new music," that is, music which in its character and substance had not existed before, cannot be the sole consideration, for all important artists have done this in all periods. Yet, the singularity of his work cannot be compared with that of any previous composer, not even with that of Richard Wagner, who quantitatively speaking, was a still greater disturber in his time. This was due, however, more to the total effect of Wagner's works through which he dominated artistically the changing temper of the European mind. Musically speaking, Wagner merely carried to its logical conclusion what Beethoven had prepared. The contention that Schönberg has also merely carried to a new or higher plane what Wagner had already established, may be true, but it is precisely this organic development which now becomes an altogether new quality and leads into a completely new sphere. While everything that has happened in music since about 1600 is based upon the system of one of the twelve major and minor keys (which our ears, conditioned through the ages, accept automatically and without conscious technical knowledge), Schönberg, after the farthest possible extension of tonal relations, conceived a music whose organic law no longer derives its relation of elements from the center of a key. To define this new conception the unhappy expression "atonal" (rejected by Schönberg himself) was formed and it has since become a meaningless, vacuous slogan, expressing a multitude of inanities and tomfoolery at which every sane man should shudder. However, on the basis of the

**81**

above and only sensible definition, it follows that the most highly publicised composers of "atonal" music really wrote little or no genuine "atonal" music. But who is aware of the fact, that it is only since about 1600 that a systematized music (in the sense of the system of major and minor tonalities) has existed, that all preceding music could, if need be, also be designated as "atonal," that one can entertain the possibility of a new, differently organized tone-language quite undisturbed. Only a person who falsely considers the established tradition of the past as the expression of an immutable law of nature, and thus unfairly mythologizes a product of the human mind, will be lost in that peculiar lamentable confusion which characterizes so many critics. Of course, the objection will be made that even if a person remains level-headed—(which, by the way, is a very commendable attitude for the contemplation of art and does not exclude genuine enthusiasm or "the overwhelming force of emotional and intellectual response through the power of thought," as Schönberg has it, but, on the contrary, makes it more than ever possible)—nevertheless his ear still remains unwilling.

This condition is not due solely to the material and purely acoustical difference of this music, but rather to its changed intellectual character which is sure to become more meaningful to future generations. For music, like other intellectual pursuits, does not manifest itself in a vacuum, nor is it divorced from the fate of the culture in which it makes its appearance, but, by its existence and struggle within the framework of this culture, it stamps its form upon it. Thus it was not possible for the post-war period, with its predominantly sociological viewpoint, to do justice to this problem, nor to analyze the intellectual function of this new music, for the simple reason that it had forced the mental realities of art, too narrowly en rapport, with the desired changes of social reality. Having emerged from a background of very primitive Marxist ideology, this enforced rapport not only missed its mark, but actually discredited itself by making the honest conservatives suspicious of the new phenomenon and by refuting its honest opponents with cheap arguments. (When anyone, such as myself, attacked it in speech or writing, he was soon labelled a reactionary). If by way of analogy we think of the change in music from the ecclesiastic tone-system to the major-minor tonalities, (which, as already stated, appeared about the 16th century and introduced the modern musical era) we shall discover evidence of a fine musicianship which, though it goes hand in hand with corresponding sociological change, functions in an atmosphere far above it. We refer to the fact that from this period dates the secularization of music, its complete emancipation from a liturgic purpose and its emergence as an autonomous art. Naturally, there had existed prior to 1600 some form of wordly music, but only from the time of the appearance of Monodie, (single melody), the opera, the stilo rappresentativo and the completely free and unused forms of symphonic and chamber music, was any real importance attached to music outside of the Church. No one denies the ecclesiastical epoch its merited admiration. It is full of the grandest creative works of the various geniuses who collectively form a single lofty range of titanic and insurmountable peaks. And it does not represent the slighest contribution to critical thought merely to observe that this noble epoch has reached an end, just as do the corresponding forms of thought and life in all fields. As in philosophy, which more and more orients itself in scholastics and in the philosophia perennis, so also in political and social circles, we are aware of a new consciousness of supernatural associations. Of course, inevitably in such times the opposition is most active and never tires of hurling false dogmas, which temporarily lay claim to a demoniacal power;—but this alone is sufficient reason for the appearance of new, powerful intellectual energy. We do not mean to be misguided when we see precisely in these new, severe boundaries and laws which Schönberg has tried to establish after stepping beyond the farthest limits of the major and minor tonalities, in order to center new focal points of definiteness in the midst of the chaos—a symbol of a new mental attitude, an attitude which in a deeper, truer sense is a conservative one and which restores to the artist genuine freedom. This doesn't mean that henceforth music must strive towards an easy submission to concrete, practical purposes. This was a mistaken short-cut of those particular sociological viewpoints to which even their deeper-minded representatives refused to subscribe however much it represented a break in ideological interpretation. The external uses, speaking in a concrete social sense, which may be destined for this new music, are not possible to foretell now, inasmuch as the new social forms themselves still remain in their primitive stages of development.

The ear of the masses, which for centuries has been increasingly accustomed to receive art, and especially music, merely as a means of entertainment, will naturally revolt for some time to come against the lack of harmony, against the seeming ugliness of modern music. Through the process of democratization and commercialization, art is subject, today as never before, to the censorship of the masses, and contemporary musical progress is necessarily accompanied by intense polemic resistance. Along with its apparent ugliness, modern music contains a great deal of genuine ugliness. It is entirely wrong and untruthful when one hears constantly repeated that it is much easier to write "atonal" music than it is to write the regular tonal. On the contrary, in modern music, which has to draw from its own sources, the lack of creative ideas becomes glaringly evident, and the listener often "senses" this "lack" because of the ineffectiveness of the music. On the other hand, music based on traditional subject-matter, even if its mental substance is weaker, always reflects some of the immortal beauty and dignity of the same subject-matter which filled the great period of classical music. It must be admitted that very few "beautiful" works of modern music exist — but never should those who dare to try to make a beginning be accused of taking things easy. The case is otherwise: a thorny path lies before them in the wilderness, and neither Arnold Schönberg nor his immediate followers will be destined to set foot in the promised land.

While here in Austria people still try to vivisect and dismiss the disturbing phenomenon, and then to close their ears to it, elsewhere in the Western World the prevalent policy is to look upon it as "old-fashioned," "out-moded," and "vieux jeu," in reaction to the time when it had been accepted very naively as fashionable and as artistically "the thing." Both attitudes are typical exhibitions of a bad conscience which is not sufficiently matured to weather the storm of scandal, and therefore tries to evade it. Surely the situation is a difficult one. and has more intellectual yardsticks than an increasingly complicated, embattled musical profession can withstand in the mere struggle for existence. A little more trust, however, may be imposed in those who, after a severe trial of conscience, have dared to venture into the unknown. Especially we Austrians, who today more than ever are conscious of how much good fortune and at the same time of how great a burden became ours to represent the vanguard of the as yet intuitively-sensed new creative forms of Western civilization, should be proud to count Arnold Schönberg as our own. In this spirit may he, who today is far from us across the ocean, practising his art, be greeted, and may he be assured of our hearty interest in his future daring adventures.

# CESAR SAERCHINGER

To justify the title of this article one would have to be a seer. The "truth" about any creative personality is not fully known for a generation or more after his death; the true value of some men's work cannot be judged for centuries. It is a little easier to say what is not the truth about a composer, and in the case of Arnold Schönberg so much obvious untruth has been spread by the scaremongers of music that it becomes a duty to rectify impressions which are obviously incorrect.

Schönberg has been called at various times an iconoclast, a sensationalist, and a lunatic. It is curious how these epithets came to be used and even believed by the credulous. Early reports of the strange character who in the last years of the nineteenth century was trying to overturn law and order in the realm of music, who in his wild ravings turned from music to painting and from painting to literature to express weird and forbidden things were only too eagerly snatched up by journalistic traffickers in novelty, and when the first works of Schö-berg made their appearance in the American concert hall they were received with something like awe. For instance, at Aeolian Hall, New York, Reinald Werrenrath, before singing some perfectly harmless early songs, actually felt contrained to reassure his public that they were really nothing to be afraid of!

Shortly after the war a young American musician, arriving in Vienna and determined to acquire the last word in morbid modernity and to breathe the air of musical wickedness, sought the acquaintance of Schön-berg. He found the master surrounded by his pupils—the advance guard of young Viennese composers—on a Sunday afternoon. He waited for the outrageous sounds; but all he heard was Mozart. Performances of Mozart quartets, under the pedantically severe surveillance of Schönberg himself!

My own first experience of Schönberg was in Amsterdam at the Mahler Festival of 1921. Here, again surrounded by his disciples, Schönberg went about, revered as a musical prophet, himself animated by only one

**90**

thought: to do homage to his own spiritual master, Gustav Mahler.

A few months later I saw Schönberg again in Vienna, ruling with the iron hand of the musical pedant, the concerts of the Society for Private Performances, insisting on innumerable rehearsals and the strictest precision and perfection in the delivery of the works of his contemporaries of all nationalities—an artistic tyranny such as I have never witnessed before or since.

These incidents may dispose of two of the epithets. Schönberg is neither a sensationalist nor a lunatic: a more conservative, a saner man, never penned notes on paper.

And what about the third? Is Schönberg an iconoclast, a futile futurist who sets out to destroy the past? Let us see.

### Schönberg the Romanticist

The futurist label was probably laid on Schönberg through lack of familiarity with his musical development and the traits which mark its successive phases. When one has made a fuller survey and has linked his work with its origins one cannot but feel that in his first period Schönberg is a romanticist definitely continuing the Wagnerian tradition; in his second stage—a more cosmopolitan one—a post-romanticist who has taken over certain traits of both Mahler and Debussy; and in his later development a musical scientist and visionary who goes back to the very genesis of music in search of a new style and a new vitality.

Instead of being recognized as further developments of a given type, the works of Strauss, Scriabin, and the early Schönberg have been successively hailed as revolutionary in their idioms. It is scarcely necessary, at this time of day, to emphasize the truism that Strauss is the continuation of Wagner. The external peculiarities of Scriabin — his scale-chord technic (which eventually landed his muse in a cul-de-sac even more restricted than the whole-tone system of Debussy) and those extra-musical features of interest which have tended to attract the non-musical rather than the musical public, made the Moscow composer seem revolutionary to the first and second decades of this century.

**92**

Similar is the case of Schönberg. Nowhere is this more apparent than when we come to works such as Verklärte Nacht. Here Tristan and the unhappy Queen of Cornwall emerge with that which the theatre sense of Wagner obscured; divested of their antique trappings, they are seen, but in that indeterminate identity which seems to be the outcome of the generalized feeling of democracy, and perhaps still more poignantly afflicted with the neurosis of modern psychology.

The superficial difference between the opera stage and the chamber concert platform, the massive Wagnerian orchestra and the finer chamber ensemble of Schönberg's sextet, may have obscured this fact for a time; but even the idiom, when boiled down to its essentials, remains the same in both cases. It is incontestably a survival of 19th-century romanticism, not even so much varied as are the romantic types of France, Russia, or Italy, but explicitly related to German idealogy.

### The Period of Expansion

The Gurrelieder, which baffled the critics largely because of the mammoth apparatus employed, remains but the epitaph of the phase inaugurated with Tristan and Isolde, to which is added the influence of Mahler, both in the spirit of the last section and the monster side-show dimensions of the score. Schönberg enlarged the heavy orchestra of Wagner by including four flutes, four piccolos, three oboes, and two English horns, three clarinets in A or B flat, two in E flat, two bass clarinets, three bassoons, two double-bassoons, ten horns, six trumpets, one bass trumpet, four tenor trombones (with one alto trombone), one bass trombone, one bass tuba, six tympani, tenor drum, side-drum, bass drum, cymbals, triangle, tam-tam, glockenspiel, xylophone, rattle, iron chains, four harps, celesta and a huge volume of strings, not to mention five solo singers, three four-part male choruses and an eight-part mixed chorus.

This is the inflated emotionalism of the romantic period pushed to its extreme. On the other hand we already see in the Gurrelieder the first signs of certain distinctive methods of Schönberg, notably those extended leaps of the melody (especially in the voice part of Tove's love song) which are later developed as a characteristic feature in the Three Piano Pieces.

But whatever the superficial radicalism of the Gurrelieder, there can be no contesting the essentially orthodox nature of the symphonic poem, Pelleas and Melisande, which follows shortly after. Here we have such polyphonic ingenuity as it would take the 16th century Netherlanders to equal, either in complexity or the turgid vagueness of the result.

## Towards Atonality

Yet while spiritually enslaved to romanticism, Schönberg even at this stage tried to break the technical fetters which bound him to the Wagnerian chariot. In the works immediately following the Gurrelieder and Verklärte Nacht he developed a hyper-chromaticism which nearly negatived tonality, made use of the whole-tone scale, introduced those "vacillating" harmonies which tend to destroy the sense of tonality, and more particularly chords consisting of super-imposed fourths. This radical departure, first noticed in the chamber symphony, is

**95**

probably what, more than anything else, stamped Schönberg as a revolutionary in people's minds.

In these transition works, culminating in the second string quartet (F-sharp minor) and the Stefan Georg songs (The Hanging Gardens), Schönberg gradually dispensed with tonality and so evolved a style which was as radically different from the old diatonic method as was Debussy's use of the whole tone scale, but much more difficult for the layman to grasp. Moreover, while Debussy's style remained predominantly homophonous, Schönberg cultivated a new kind of counterpoint, and, as a natural consequence, discarded the old, essentially harmonic, conceptions of consonance and dissonance.

The first string quartet, definitely classical in form, already shows tendencies to atonality, but also betrays Schönberg's uncertainty at this period in its diatonic platitudes and the conventional cadences with which many otherwise daring passages conclude. Inversely, simple melodic phrases culminate in curious passages destroying all feeling of tonic centrality or dispersing into vagueness.

The Chamber Symphony, opus 9, shows kindred uncertainty. It has more unity within itself, but its form is much less cleanly cut or defined. All in all, it remains a fascinating mosaic of themes, but these are not treated with the contrapuntal skill of which the composer is capable; nor, paradoxically, is the development of the work anything that can be recognized as symphonic. Indeed, here one finds Schönberg attempting to create a sense of homogeneity by the reiterated recurrence of themes only, a style which is more arabesque than symphonic. The Chamber Symphony, incidentally, marks the start of the modern bent towards the chamber-orchestral form in Germany.

It is immediately followed by the F-minor string quartet, in the last two movements of which Schönberg adds a soprano voice—in much the same way as Mahler employed the human voice in his symphonies—singing ecstatically of "other worlds" in the verses of Stefan Georg. In the last movement, appropriately enough, we have the first definitely "atonal" passages of any length. The quartet with its hyper-romanticism (of a very beautiful kind) signalizes the end of Schönberg's first "period" — largely a period of "expansion." A new chapter opens, which by contrast might be called a period of contraction.

### The Period of Contraction

There exists a kind of neurosis following on super-emotionalism which, while it differs radically on the surface, is really the outcome of the same psychological elements. This is the case with romanticism and the decadence into which it fell. Wagner suffered from a tendency to over-statement, an effusion of emotion. The second phase of Schönberg signalizes the decline of Wagnerian-Straussian romanticism into the painful contraction of emotion, the sense of over-poignancy and morbidity into which romantic feeling falls when its first erotic and emotional impulses have worn themselves out. This is the keynote of Schönberg's subsequent work.

Added, is the rather symptomatic trait of mysticism which is revealed in the libretto of his oratorio, Jacob's Ladder, for it is in the nature of decadence to seek to revive the romantic thrill in exploring the macabre, the obscure and the vaguely visionary.

The Hanging Gardens, the fifteen poems of Georg set in a cycle by Schönberg, are a blossoming of this neurotic flower. Here already worn romantic emotion seeks the extremities of painfulness and of poignancy to find a new sensation. In Herzgewächse, opus 20, we have the climax of this. Here the soprano part is laid out for a voice capable of three octaves. Here, also, we have a deliberate seeking for the almost sadistically acute jarring of the voice line with the accompaniment.

In the three piano pieces, opus 11, we see the first stirrings of this neurotic and essentially personal style, which has laid the foundations of the Viennese school. The Five Orchestral Pieces, opus 16, continue it in the domain of the orchestra. They explore—with fine sensibility, be it said—the whole range of individualization in orchestral writing, which in modern music has taken the place of group combinations. This is Schönberg's outstanding contribution to modern orchestral development. But the composer does not limit himself to the domain of sensitive expression. He explores with the feeling of a scientist in a laboratory, testing new, attenuated compounds of chemical ingredients.

Pierrot Lunaire, a triple cycle of twenty-one poems by Albert Giraud (translated by Erich Hartleben) marks the neurotic apex of Schönberg's development. Here is that seeking after the super-sensual and the macabre which marks so much of that decadence which one finds in the ultra-romantic genius of E. T. A. Hoffmann in literature. Sardonic, sadistic, agonizing, cynically humorous, diabolical and tenderly sentimental by turns, this is essentially romantic music, lacerating its spirit by throwing harsh lights of analysis upon itself.

Technically, Pierrot marks the full development of Schönberg's ultra-expressive style, with its zig-zag melody of wide skips, its exploitation of the tone color of individual instruments, its use of independent atonal counterpoint and its extreme economy of harmonic means joined to a highly poignant use of acute dissonance. Together with the second F-sharp minor quartet it also is the high-water mark of the composer's inspiration, in so far as the "romantic" Schönberg is concerned.

The monodrama, Erwartung, which preceded it, and the symbolical music drama, Die Glückliche Hand, which followed it, are imbued with the overpoignant emotionalism of this middle period. From a practical point of view they are hardly more than dramatic experiments, though of a highly interesting kind.

### The Third Period

The notion of Schönberg as a neurotic post-romanticist would no doubt predominate in posterity's estimate, had there not occurred a second decisive change in the composer's outlook. His "second period" in which he evolved his own idiom by a deliberate change of his musical fabric, we have called a period of contraction. The third, beginning like the second with a work for the piano (Five Pieces, opus 23) is a period of concentration and systematization. In this period Schönberg attempts to provide the stylistic forces which he dissolved in his previous works with new centers of gravity—new unifying elements.

When he discarded the harmonic style Schönberg also had to abandon the essentially harmonic or "tonal" principles of form. In searching for others he logically went back to a time when music was as essentially polyphonic as his own. In Pierrot Lunaire one song, Die Nacht, is a passacaglia, and another, Der Mondfleck, contains a "crab canon"—a favorite form with the contrapuntists of the 16th century. Now, in his third period, Schönberg discards this retrogressive tendency, and aims to establish a new theory of composition, which he calls Twelve-Tone Music.

Roughly, the "twelve-tone" style is synonymous with complete atonality—a state in which all the twelve tones of the chromatic scale are of equal importance. But constant equality means monotony (as Debussy's whole-tone style has proved), and in order to differentiate, a new kind of limitation becomes necessary. Schönberg therefore selects a number of tones from the twelve and places them in a definite melodic order. The sequence may be inverted, and in either its original form or its inversion it may be reversed, crab-fashion. This gives four varieties, and these again may be transposed to any part of the scale. Also they may be used vertically, in quasi-harmonies or tone-clusters. Thus unity and variety—form and development—are achieved.

## Theory and Practice

That is the theory. Whether any ordinary ear can, or will ever learn to, distinguish these relationships, or whether they will impose themselves subconsciously on the human mind as have the arbitrary relationships of our own tempered scale tonalities, will be seen only by the next generation.

Schönberg has written, in accordance with these self-imposed doctrines, the works of his third period, representative of a neoclassicism that is obviously more academic than the classicism with which we are familiar. Enough of them have been analyzed by one of his pupils for us to know that they are constructed according to the system. They include the five piano pieces, opus 23, and the piano suite, opus 25; the serenade for seven instruments (clarinet, bass clarinet, mandolin, guitar, violin, viola and 'cello, plus a bass voice in one of the movements); the quintet for wind instruments, opus 27; and the third string quartet, opus 29, also Theme Variations for orchestra, opus 30, which aroused protest from a New York audience when it was performed under Stokowski.

That the presence of this system need not militate against the sensuous appeal of the music was proved to the present writer by the Serenade, opus 24, when it was performed at the International Festival in Venice four years ago. Its bitter-sweet melancholy still shows a relationship to Pierrot Lunaire, but in his new classical mood the composer seems to have stripped off the last vestiges of that hyper-emotionalism which savored so definitely of decadence.

### Not an Iconoclast

If proof were still needed, this last phase of Schönberg's development proves that he is anything but an iconoclast. Not to tear down but to build up new laws in place of those which have evaporated under his very hands—that is his aim. One of his contemporaries—no need to mention names—has compared his method to the methods of modern surgery. The phrase "professor of modernity" has probably been coined for him. Not radicalism but academicism is the charge levelled at Schönberg by his colleagues today.

How are we to account for it? Analysis, the hall-mark of the self-searching romanticist, is the key to Schönberg's musical identity. Here is the academic by inclination, the scientist of music, at first expressing his natural bent in laboratory experiments in musical media, then turning to the analysis of moods in the manner of the Viennese psycho-analytical school, and finally in the analysis of his own idiom.

As a great analyst, as a great laboratory worker in music, Schönberg must stand. As a composer he has not only added a colossal footnote to the past phase of Romanticism, but has opened up new paths upon which others are already advancing. For them there is no turning back. If Schönberg has done anything he has done this: he has destroyed the mawkish romanticism and the tepid impressionism of the last century with the acid of his intellect. The mediocrities of tomorrow must at least spare us the agonies of yesterday's clichés.

But all this does not dispose of the problem. Schönberg at the age of fifty-four is still the most problematical figure in contemporary music. Revered by his followers as no other living master, adorned with the halo of a musical saint, he is less recognized in a material way— by successful performances—than any other composer of prominence, including some of those who are his disciples. In other words, the principles which he himself has enunciated have been utilized by others with more material success than by himself. Others, less respected, are more applauded. Others, whose artistic creeds are still not definitely formed, have shown a vitality in the use of the new idiom which makes Schönberg appear weak by comparison.

Are we to assume that Schönberg, preoccupied with the blazing of a new trail, has left the cultivation of the wilderness to others? Or are those right who, while respecting his great intellectual powers, deny him the essential quality of genius—the elemental creative force?

**106**

That is, and will be, the problem for some time to come. It will be answered by others besides ourselves, and only when it is answered will the "truth about Schönberg" be known.

[1930]

**107**

# RICHARD BUHLIG

Arnold Schoenberg has been the subject of much discussion as a musical innovator, as the composer, who more than any of his contemporaries, has taken music into realms hitherto unknown. Much has been written regarding the nature of his "new" tonal medium and for and against "atonality," which has been associated principally with his name. The opponents of atonality have asserted that tonality is inherent in the very nature of music. The supporters of atonality have stated, in the words of Schoenberg, that "tonality is not an eternal law of music, but simply a means toward the achievement of musical form," and by inference, that atonality is another.

The discussions have continued, more recently, concerning his "twelve-tone-music," the "tone-rows." These are ordered successions of the twelve half-tones as a basis for composition, a modus operandi, an imposed discipline of tonal relationships. This discipline was,

**109**

doubtless, intuitively found, even though afterwards intellectually controlled. It was necessary because the "grammar" of the old diatonic relationships must of necessity lose its validity in atonal music with its absence of a tonic as a gravitational center.

To the bewildered layman it might seem that this music is a complete volte-face, that it has severed all connection with the music of the past, and that, whereas the development of our tonal resources, up to this point, could be traced by steps of logical growth, now all direction had been lost. Nothing could, however, be farther from the truth.

Schoenberg's "innovation" is a perfectly logical step, the next logical step in the development of our tonal resources. It may be a turning in the road, but that is where the road turns. The road is still the same. And, although this turning may seemingly lead into a strange new land, it is the one road, traveled from the beginning of our music in regard to its material, which has led there.

This material, first modal, then diatonic, progressively

**110**

absorbs into itself the auxiliary, the chromatic, tones, which it uses with ever greater freedom. But even when the extremest limits of freedom are reached, as in our own time, these tones still remain chromatic, accessory to a diatonic or "tonal" basis, and subordinated to it. As chromaticism they are *color* over underlying diatonic *form*. When, as at some time they must, having become so powerful, these chromatic tones wrest to themselves equal importance with the diatonic substratum, they are chromatic no longer, and the gravitational center of a tonic disappears. With it, of necessity, also disappears the concept of dissonance relative to consonance. This is the turning in the road which he, who having traveled thus far, and being impelled to go on, must, of necessity, take.

Schoenberg has felt this necessity. In this respect he *has* created a "new" music, but new only as today is new, born out of all the yesterdays behind it, and belonging to them in an unbroken sequence.

Schoenberg has not sought this new thing. He has not "invented" any more than any creative musician before

**111**

him has invented. Step by step this evolution of our tonal language has proceeded intuitively from the need of creative musicians. It is for theory to explain it afterward. (In this regard it is significant to note that Schoenberg, in his "Harmonielehre" gives examples of new harmonic progressions, stating that he knows these are "right," without, however, yet being able to explain their "rightness.")

Schoenberg has never striven for originality. Nothing could be farther from this man's music, so simple in its rectitude and uncompromising in its sincerity. Neither has he conformed to any aesthetic theory of beauty. He has striven for truth, the truth of his own nature, and he has had no choice. Inner necessity is the mother of art, and the artist impelled by this necessity and "realizing," (the word is Cézanne's), creates beauty, beauty as a by-product, as it were, something which he did not set out to find. For who shall know what beauty is? Aesthetics can demonstrate it afterwards from the living works of music. Every great piece of music has a first-timeness, a something which never was before. It is always new music. But again it is timeless. We recognize an enduring idea which is at the heart of all great music, relating it in unbroken continuity.

•

Tradition is a word from which we, so conscious of our "modernism," are apt to recoil, prone, as we are, to regard tradition as a conservation of the dead-wood of the past, a past which we think to have done with. Tradition is, however, a living thing, a handing-on, as the word signifies, a transmission of that which endures through all change, and which, enduring, relates all manifestations to each other in the living continuity mentioned above.

The enduring Idea in the great tradition of music is the *primacy of form,* objectivation through form. Form is not formula, although it becomes that in the dreary wastes of "academic" art—a recipe to be taught and imitated. Neither is form structure. "Form is act," creative act. Structure is its visibility. "Form is soul and doth the body make." It is this primacy of form "realized" which is the signature of all great music, of music

**113**

which achieves its essential nature. This, its nature, imposes that music be music only, never adjunct or illustration of something else, that all extra-musical elements from which it may have proceeded be distilled in the alembic of form, nothing remaining but a complex of significant, because necessary, purely musical relationships.

Schoenberg is today the outstanding representative of this great tradition. He has not arrived here through intellectual search. There has been with him no return to the past, no "back-to-the-classics," no effort toward "objective" music. He has never turned back. All past achievement, its great tradition,—these things are his by natural right and he has gone forward possessing these things as his own. He never had any formal training, being almost entirely self-taught. His teachers have been the great masters, his kin and kind, and his profound insight into their works has been his school, as these works are his conscious inheritance. He has gone his way simply and directly, unballasted by false deductions from the past and unbewildered by new theories and "isms." His

**114**

work has always been the expression of that which is essential to music—that music be music alone, determined only by its musical substance.

It might seem that there were early deviations from this path. His music, later so free from all extra-musical and literary elements, includes early works like "Die Verklaerte Nacht" with a literary background, the "Pelleas," a symphonic poem,—works where extra-musical elements were an impulse toward creation. But the created work has shed them and music existing wholly through its form remains. Schubert songs and Mozart operas are "pure" music. The music has absorbed the text, the action, and never becomes illustration. This may seem difficult to understand. It is because, to quote Schoenberg's essay on the relation of music to a text, "there are only relatively few people who are capable of understanding, purely musically, what music has to say."

It is comprehensible that a listener, first hearing one of Schoenberg's later works, might ask, in perplexity where this realization of form, which manifests as significant, because necessary, relationships, is to be found. It is true that its presence might be difficult to perceive, but this is due wholly to the unwontedness of Schoenberg's tonal language. Such situations have recurred often in the history of music. We know of epoch-making works which were first heard as disorder and musical non-sense, except by a few discerning ears, works which contain for us in the highest degree all those qualities which were denied them by contemporary listeners. Moreover, personal experience confirms this statement. The present writer well remembers a performance in Berlin, a mere twenty-five years ago, of Schoenberg's first string quartet, a performance which roused a riot of abuse and antagonism, and at which the composer, who was present, was all but assaulted. To the musical listener of today this work no longer presents any problems which could stand in the way of recognizing it for what it is, a work of musical invention unequalled by any contemporary composer, and proceeding from the classical string quartet. What has happened? It is we, who, in the intervening years, have come to it, not it to us. It has not moved.

**116**

Is it therefore too daring to predict that the fourth quartet, Schoenberg's most recent work, will be as clear to listeners of the next generation, and that they will recognize in it, to an even greater degree perhaps, that clarity and concentration of form which constitutes it a work in the great tradition, and for all its differences, relates it to the quartets of Beethoven? It is necessary to say this in order to make Schoenberg's position clear to us, his contemporaries, for, to a later generation such clarification will not be needed. They will see in him a man, who, in a time of much uncertain groping and aimless following of ephemeral gods, quietly kept the flame burning, and handed it on to the future.

His works exist, they are there for posterity, regardless of contemporary recognition of their importance. New works are being created. His place in the present, a living link between past and future, has long been recognized by a band of ardent young spirits, his pupils. Even at a time when he was still unknown to the world, they followed him, enriched by his vast knowledge, and finding their own way by the light of his genius.

**117**

Schoenberg is now in America and his activity as a teacher continues in our midst, a fact of incalculable importance for our young school of composers.

Beyond this immediate influence on his pupils, something in the very nature of the man should be of deepest import for the whole of our musical life—his conception of the arduous responsibility of the artist and the inviolability of music.

[1936]

**118**

# ERWIN STEIN

Musical thought and sound become one in creative art. But sometimes it is a long way from the thought to the creation of the sound by means of which it is expressed; likewise for the listener by way of his apperception, it is a long way from the sound to the comprehension of the thought.

Sound is the outward manifestation of music; not the goal but the result. In itself it has no musical meaning. Sounds may be pleasing according to the opinion of the listener but if he demands a special kind of sound he shows a complete misunderstanding of the nature of music. Nevertheless he may be able to give an opinion in a concrete sense on some points of a work for the sound is adequate as an expression of the thought.

Every master has his own sound world which corresponds to his individual nature and by means of which he expresses his thoughts. These vary radically from time to time so that our contemporaries find it difficult to

**119**

apperceive the new sound and by means of it reach the thought.

The new thought and the new sound are so closely interwoven that sometimes the composer himself hardly knows if they were not conceived simultaneously.

Schoenberg wrote "For the first time in my songs after the poems of Georg I approached the expression of an ideal which had been hovering around me for years." The listener also was astonished at this new sound. It was as if a new dimension had been contacted. Contours became apparent that scarcely seemed in the realm of music and in this strange new light the finest gradations of psychical experience were perceptible. This music soared outside the limits of any note values as if time itself had ceased to flow.

Clear-cut rhythmic figures were combined with chords creating sound pictures of almost torturing intensity. Above this accompaniment the voice floated following the natural rise and fall of speech in melodies of undreamed of tenderness and beauty. In this manner the Georg songs impressed us. Of course there were listeners who only remarked the absence of familiar landmarks. There were no concords, no triads and no fixed tonality. But the lack of all these resulted in an extremely positive quality. The music contained richer sounds and fuller harmonies while the tonality expanded into the infinite. One might ask if dissonance is as apt for artistic expression as consonance but it is in its very nature far more expressive.

Schoenberg has proved this to us for all time by his use of it in moments of greatest emotion. The intensity created by dissonance does not consist in that it is resolved but rather in the fact that it is allowed to sound.

Regarding the oft-repeated effect of discord followed by its resolution, it is the first of the two that is by far the more interesting. It is as if the simple harmonies dissolved or spread like light in the prism, reuniting again with the resolution. Let us then have the dissonance unresolved recognizing that it is far more colorful than any nicely constructed consonance. In this sense Schoenberg's sound is real polyphony.

Formerly parallel octaves and fifths were forbidden because they contributed nothing new and could not even be considered as counterpoint. Now the same thing happened with the triad. It is understood and does not need to be affirmed. It contains only the first overtones and like the fifths and octaves it makes no counterpoint. It is merely a unison—only able to unite and not to differentiate.

Schoenberg's part writing consists in that the parts do not mingle one with another. Each voice sings individually. Each note has its own life and enriches the whole by moving according to its own laws. It is the same in polyphonic writing. Here the whole sound is enriched by each voice singing its individual melody. Dissonance lightens (clarifies) the vertical sound and elucidates the thought in polyphonic writing.

Schoenberg's mode of expression is established by means of his sound world and in this way he speaks clearly and with the utmost concentration. Since writing these songs Schoenberg has put his ideas in shorter forms thus experimenting in his use of the new sounds. These were at first insufficient for symphonic works of large struct-

**122**

ure. By shattering the tonal center the large form was destroyed.

With the birth of the twelve-tone series (row), the newly-oriented co-ordination took the place of the old tonal system and Schoenberg realized his ideal of creating large works in his own manner. The new sounds born of the need for a new mode of expression were now moulded into tangible material.

[1934]

123

# EDUARD STEUERMANN

It would appear that Schoenberg has most frequently written for the piano when a particularly important step had to be taken in the development that so thoroughly changed the very foundations of musical structure. Almost all of his compositions for the piano are milestones in the development of modern music, and it is important first to examine them from that point of view.

Schoenberg's first compositions for the piano are the pieces Op. 11, and judging from the opus number, his first work in which the dissolution of tonality has been thoroughly accomplished. Moreover, the third piece of this series is the first one in which Schoenberg's musical form takes an entirely new road. Abandoning all provable thematics, this piece builds to a climax by freely unfolding its inner musical spirit. Here it is left to coming generations to *prove* to what extent thematics or motivics have remained obligatory, and in what way the structure follows the eternal laws of musical creation. For us it is sufficient to feel the power and the logic of this musical language, and to look upon this work as pure "expression," fulfilling laws that have not yet been discovered.

In the first and the second pieces of Op. 11 we can still recognize the continuation of the previous methods of formulation; their expression, however far apart from everything hitherto known, establishes them as the prototype of the Schoenberg piano piece.

Another factor, so characteristic of the development of music through Schoenberg, is of special importance to the cycle Op. 19—*brevity*. "Aphoristic," "sketchy," etc., were the expressions in the reviews of these compositions. One would be mistaken, however, who sees in these works the mere abbreviation of musical thoughts or fragments of them. On the contrary, these are musical organisms having their own particular dimensions, which are permitted to live their rich and full life. The concentration of the expression of the musical thought, the avoidance of superfluous repetitions, especially such as might strengthen the feeling of tonality are here the important components of the development of this style into the "method of the twelve-tone composition."

Two pieces seem especially characteristic to me: the first which, although composed of varied and heterogeneous elements, still shows the long-drawn line of the "eternal melody." And the last, essentially consisting of one single chord, which, together with the third of the "Five pieces for orchestra" Op. 16, is something unique in the realm of music.

Those who, in the development of Schoenberg's "dissonant" style of music (as shown, for instance, in his compositions "ERWARTUNG" and "GLUECK LICHE HAND"), have seen the climax of his achievement, were probably surprised when it became apparent that the end of the road was still far off. The period of seeming "dissolution" was to be followed by a period of reorganization and· demarcation, that is, the "method of composition with twelve tones." In this connection, Schoenberg's work entitled "Five pieces for the piano, Op. 23" published by Hansen in Kopenhagen, seems particularly important. We realize that in these pieces the principles on which the

127

"method of twelve-tone compositions" is based are first fully expressed. After the exposition of the long-extended main theme, the second part of the first piece employs, perhaps for the first time, a new *"principle of repetition."* It is the resumption of the tones of a theme, while at the same time the rhythm and the octave-position of these notes are changed. So, the "expression" can lead from the original one to distant spheres, without the theme loosing its "identity." Today, after years have passed this technique has, through Schoenberg and the composers who follow him, become a matter of course. Therefore we easily forget that here we are confronted by a creative act of rare originality and significance.

Another method of composition is recognizable in the second piece, namely the condensation into one chord of consecutively sounded melodic tones. This might be called *thematic harmony.* While indications of it appear earlier (see "Passacaglia" from "Pierrot Lunaire") here this principle is expressed *clearly* for the first time, and confirms the thematic equivalence of the horizontal and the vertical.

**128**

A further development of this style produces the Piano-Suite Op. 25. Here Schoenberg's interest for the older forms and types, and also their possibilities for modern music, are shown for the first time. This trait of his musical nature makes his later rearrangements of the works of Handel and Monn understandable. For us, these works rather serve to indicate the close affinity of Schoenberg's music to the classical. Whenever the struggles of a period of development are over, the conception of the unity of art is once more impressed upon us.

The following compositions for the piano: the piano piece Op. 33a, and the one published by ''New Music'' present to us, in a sense, once again the two poles of expression of Schoenberg's language. Op. 33a, composed of contrasting elements, frequently sounding as if ''disrupted,'' and the other, a quietly flowing ''Song Without Words'' which, in leisurely abandon, gives us all the nuances of the musical thought.

There is a great deal to be said about Schoenberg's piano style. It originates from the classical, and in his earlier works (song accompaniments), is sometimes reminiscent of Brahms. But soon it developed the same originality that characterizes all manifestations of his spirit.

The essence of Schoenberg's piano style, like the essence of his entire musical thinking, is *polyphony*. This polyphony is dissolved into an endless succession of pianistic ideas, constantly changing, repeating themselves only occasionally; and only very seldom remaining sufficiently unchanged to form extended sequences of the same pianistic structure. (This by the way, occurs more often in Schoenberg's later works).

One might say that a piano piece compares with a piece for the orchestra as drawing to a painting. A piece for the piano does not possess definite "colours." and has to express its power in its own way. With Schoenberg the "color effect" does not originate, as in the romantic piano music, from the repetition of the thought in different variations, octave positions, duplications. etc. No, it is not an adornment of, but something that can not be separated from the essential "thought"; it is something that develops and changes *with* the thought.

The pianist is apt to form his musical conception of a composition from its instrumental aspect. With Schoenberg, he must perform quite a bit of mental work beforehand: one could hardly approach this music without previous conception. First, he must pianistically understand (and not misunderstand) every single idea of the piece. Second, he must be able to build up these different ideas into one fluent stream of music. Third, he must do justice to that melodic-polyphonic element, which, to my feeling, is the very essence of Schoenberg's music.

Also, for the interpretation of his piano compositions a considerable mastery of the technique of phrasing is necessary. Phrased inadequately a classical melody might only be less beautiful, whereas Schoenberg's would be downright incomprehensible. In this connection, the feeling for the new intervals is also of importance. The width of the interval-span, must not destroy the feeling for their relation, and only the most delicate sensitivity for the weight or lightness of the stresses and releases

**131**

enables one to speak this language. The treatment of harmonies, the art of shaping a melody with its differentiations between principal and secondary voices—all these things require most of all, a conception of the composition as a whole.

Is it necessary to discuss the position of Schoenberg's work? Or the problems they offer to the listener? For the problem of their understanding is the problem of art itself. At a time when the spread of entertainment music has assumed such vast proportions, it might prove difficult even for the genuine music lover to find the proper perspective of art. Only those to whom it is a necessity will be able to muster the required concentration. A piece of art demands to be explored, to the best ability of the art lover; it must be contemplated from all angles; must be followed when it hurries you, and must be gazed at quietly when it calls a halt. The thrill of the unexperienced (a trait of entertainment sensationalism) is not the point: here surprise is only what we have expected. These are the prerequisites of *all* enjoyment of true art: when measured with these measurements, the unusualness of Schoenberg's music does not offer greater difficulties than any other work of art that one desires to take seriously. Much has been said about understanding and appreciation of music. In art to understand means to love, and I do not believe, that in the last analysis, there exists another explanation.

If today Schoenberg's work appears somewhat "isolated," then this is exactly the thing that lifts it into a sphere where it can not be touched by the commonplace. This very isolation amidst the changing and passing of everyday phenomena will make his music endure.

[1937]

133

# JOSÉ RODRIGUEZ

In the summer of 1917, while Horne's First Army
was busy making itself at home on the Oppy-Mericourt
front after a tedious and disagreeable journey from
Arras and Souchez, the thumb and forefinger of Provi-
dence lifted me from the company of that pilgrimage and
deposited me in the neighborhood of Doullens for a de-
licious holiday that was technically called a Course in
Enemy Weapons. The favorite retreat for students at
the time was a canteen where, if one were eccentric, one
could write letters, sing songs, lose one's pay at Crown
and Anchor or barter regimental gossip; the conventional
spirits, on the other hand, merely courted the fugitive
Nirvana usually found after carefully scrutinizing the
bottoms of a variable number of glasses.

One afternoon — school often adjourned early — I
strolled in to find a very young officer of the Seaforth
Highlanders sitting at the piano and drawing from its
vitals some very strange harmonies. This was my first

**135**

meeting with the music of Arnold Schoenberg. The young officer was Caryl Wood, digitally an indifferent pianist, but with a superb memory and sensitive musicality, who could quote almost any work at least for a few bars and whose taste leaned toward the *curiosa* of the art. As such he had collected several excerpts from Schoenberg's Op. 11, which he played over and over again interspersed among bits of Debussy, Franck, Reger and Scriabine. Just as this was my first hearing of notes by Schoenberg, it was also my introduction to the Schoenberg legend. Briefly, this is that Schoenberg is merely a cerebralist, an experimenter, a laboratory mole, a mathematician, an originator and compiler of tortuous theories. Wood was no silly Chauvinist, so his animus against Schoenberg was not founded on the then popular notion that there was no balm in Gilead nor in any point between the British and Russian fronts. But he had imbibed his notions from London musical circles, which were at that time in full cry, with insular determination and primness, against all heresies that threatened the musico-esthetic heritage of Mendelssohn and Handel.

Always excited and even fascinated by any expression that menaced the composure of sacred cows, I was delighted with the spoonfuls of Schoenberg that Wood doled out. Arduous chores in the vicinity of Paschaendale in the months immediately following, and the problems of post-bellum readjustment prevented my closer acquaintance with the music. In 1920 came out a volume of readable and often acute characterizations by Paul Rosenfeld — Musical Portraits — where I read that "Schoenberg is the great troubling presence of modern music. His vast, sallow skull lowers over it like a sort of North Cape. For with him, with the famous cruel five orchestral and nine piano pieces, we seem to be entering the Arctic zone of musical art. . . . One finds the experimental and methodical at every turn. . . . Behind them one seems invariably to perceive some one sitting before a sheet of music paper and tampering with the art of music; seeking to discover what would result were he to accept as harmonic basis not the major triad but the major ninth, to set two contradictory rhythms clashing, or to sharpen everything and maintain a geometric hardness of line. . . .

**137**

They smell of the synagogue as much as they do of the laboratory. Beside the Doctor of Music there stands the Talmudic Jew, the man all intellect and no feeling, who subtilizes over musical art as though it were the Law."

That decided me. I must know something first-hand of Arnold Schoenberg; and I went much further than most critics, for I actually studied some of his scores, carefully listened to recorded performances of the music, and even strained my anemic German enough to read his Harmonielehre. Knowing fully from the frequent pronouncements of my betters that I was a creature of no intellect and all feeling, assured by centuries of family records that I was not a Talmudic Jew, and being equally sure that I was not and never could be a Doctor of Music, I was astonished to find that Schoenberg's music produced in me a distinct pleasure, a warmth and awareness, a quickening of my musical faculties. At first I suspected myself and afterward, with better cause, suspected the protagonists of the Schoenberg legend.

Later on I was thrown into the company of Schoenberg. I have known long enough that personal association has a tendency to promote favorable bias; also that there are no men of genius but only works of genius. The best of any artist is in his work; there we receive the quintessence of his excellence, the cream of his thought. The man himself is usually disappointing. I forget what wit once remarked that meeting a celebrity was like one's first love; one felt afterward like asking, is that all? So when meeting and talking with Schoenberg I was strictly on the defensive; and it required long months to persuade myself that to study and understand the incubus that legend has made of Schoenberg, it was also necessary to know the man.

It is a natural temptation for critics to engage in speculations more calculated to display their learning or virtuosity than to give a clear, dispassionate and accurate idea of their subject. Consequently, most critical writing, specially about music, proves sterile and misleading. Critics, to my mind, should be missionaries and prophets whose function is to discover and share with humanity the delightful secret that is music. Good missionaries are rare; good dissectionists are a drug on the market. To the devil then, I say, with pseudo-profundities and legends; or, if your taste is for real profundities, to Erwin Stein, to Paul Bekker, to Dr. Egon Wellesz, to Dr. Paul Stefan, to D. I. Bach with you. I shall remain, as I was a day or so ago, with Arnold Schoenberg, chatting quietly by his fireside after the baby, against all her cajoling objections (she looks like a Cherokee rose), has been put to bed.

Let us take, one by one, the usual decisions concerning Schoenberg's music, beginning with the most widespread and popular: That there is "no beauty, no emotion, no warmth, in it." I believe that if it were possible to pluck from their seats in a concert hall various specimens of the sub-species *music-lover* and mention to them the name Arnold Schoenberg, they would nine times out of ten utter that representative squeak, adding "besides, I don't like it."

Now it is quite impossible to argue with a man about what he likes or what he doesn't like. Some people are excessively fond of parsnips and I detest them. I can perhaps be convinced that parsnips may be good for the digestion or the complexion; nevertheless I shall still loathe them. Neither is it possible, without writing a treatise on esthetic, to undertake definition of such terms as *emotion* and *beauty*. If the anti-Schoenbergian says that to him the music is *cold,* he must continue to shiver; if his emotional nature is unsatisfied, he must remain unslaked. I cannot argue his feelings away. His feelings are his own and only he can answer for them, or for their absence. But when he says that the music *has not* warmth, emotion or beauty, he is uttering the same kind of nonsense I should be if I denied the nutritive value or the palatability of parsnips—to other people. Furthermore, I have tasted parsnips; the chief objectors that I personally know against Schoenberg, have heard little if any of his music.

There is also the puzzling question as to where *feeling* ends and *intellect* begins. I do piously wish there were a definite, an unquestionable frontier between the two; that each refrained from infiltrating into the other's territory; that we could all say ''now I am all feeling'' and then, a moment afterward ''now I am all intellect.'' But alas, the complexity of our natures, as well as the complexity of music, does not allow of such psychic black-and-white. There are, in all music, moments of supreme ecstasy when the faculty of thought seems suspended and we live in a celestial eternity; in Palestrina, Bach, Mozart, Beethoven, Chopin, Franck and Schoenberg. But if we examine for an instant the body of the thought, we see that intellect, ingenuity and craftsmanship are inseparable and essential elements of the total effect. When a person, however, has succeeded in pigeonholing his reactions, it is beyond hope to consider music from a scientific or at least logical point of view.

I said some things to this effect to Schoenberg recently. He listened to me with an attentive smile, a patient smile. His dark and lively eyes, his mobile features, his well-modelled head tipped to one side—this is the ''vast, sallow skull'' of Rosenfeld—he said:

''Yes,'' sighing, ''I am unfortunately considered according to the legends of biographers. This is an absurdity, but I suppose an unavoidable absurdity. I am still waiting to be judged according to my music. My work should be judged as it enters the ears and heads of *listeners,* not as it is described to the eyes of *readers.*"

RODRIGUEZ: That is reasonable enough. I have been singing the same song. But you remember the struggle we had with your concerts recently. There seems to be an official apathy, or perhaps opposition, to the proper rehearsal, presentation and exploitation of the music. Consequently, when it is performed, even in extremely modest doses, few people know about it, and fewer still attend. The proportion of those who listen is still smaller.

SCHOENBERG: I have wished this was not true. But I am convinced of it. However, opposition is nothing new to one who wishes to say something new or something old in a new way. The history of music is a collected record of such oppositions. Here in Los Angeles, however, the antagonism has been very mild and below the surface. At first, particularly when my first string quartet appeared, there were actual fist fights in the audience.

RODRIQUEZ: If we could only have had a riot ourselves, a nice little riot, a modest bit of a brawl! We

**143**

could have filled the house later on without trouble and the publicity would be automatic!

SCHOENBERG: Now about this matter of emotion, of inspiration—eh?

RODRIGUEZ: Oh, yes.

SCHOENBERG: It might astonish some critics that I am somewhat the creature of inspiration. I compose and paint instinctively. When I am not in the mood, I cannot even write a good example in harmony for my pupils. There are times when I write with the greatest fluency and ease. My third string quartet was composed in six weeks. They say I am a mathematician! Mathematics goes much slower.

RODRIGUEZ: We have at least one consolation. I describe it thus: Concepts of beauty are conventions that change with the times. What is to us familiar and most acceptable in Beethoven, Wagner and Debussy was in their day hateful to their contemporaries. I wonder what Mozart would have thought of Chopin's modulations!

SCHOENBERG: Mozart would have considered them fantastic, awkward, crude and artificial, naturally. But

**144**

time is a great conqueror. He will bring understanding to my works; indeed, he already has. No one is shocked nowadays by my Verklarte Nacht. Even last week, when my last string quartet was played by the Kolisch ensemble, it was heard with some enthusiasm, and a respect that to me brought the sudden and astonishing thought: "Heavens, am I being popularly accepted at last?"

RODRIGUEZ: Of course, as far as understanding in time is concerned—

SCHOENBERG: Even Mozart is hard to understand sometimes, if one really listens. I have often been puzzled when hearing some Mozart work for the first time.

The conversation veered toward the matter of the twelve-tone scale. I had known that Schoenberg had for a long time been considering a companion work to his Harmonielehre: Composition mit zwölf tönen. I had also read Stein's exposition of the twelve-tone system in his Neue Formprinzipien (Von Neuer Musik; Cologne, 1925). And, to save my life I could notice nothing in the so-called system that was anything more than an extension and increase of the material available to the composer. I had communicated my notion to Joseph Achron, also timidly advancing the opinion that to understand Schoenberg one should really first understand the sixteenth-century contrapuntists. I was not certain of my ground; I had not disputed with the doctors long enough to realize that my weakness was my strength. The incident was curious, for Achron had some time before said the same things, unknown to me.

SCHOENBERG: That is correct. Stein, of course, speaks only of technical methods, which are always overrated.

RODRIGUEZ: Let me expose myself further. I believe that the twelve-tone scale was predicted and sometimes unconsciously used by men like Chopin. I have even felt that Beethoven foreshadowed atonality.

SCHOENBERG: You must be thinking of the sonata *Les Adieux* and the Eroica.

RODRIGUEZ: Yes, have you the score?

We went to the piano and I turned to the first movement of the Eroica, where the violins shiver on the A-flat and B-flat of the dominant seventh chord while the first horn enters with the principal subject in the tonic.

SCHOENBERG: This, in my opinion, is a mistake. It was meant to be in B-flat.

He played the passage, transposing the horn-theme into the dominant of E-flat. I had in mind an objection, that since the Eroica was performed many times during Beethoven's life and since he had every opportunity of correcting the passage, he had not done so, thus confirming his intention. But there were other things at hand to talk about. A curious incident!

RODRIGUEZ: You tell me you are a creature of inspiration. Give me some idea of the process you follow.

SCHOENBERG: I see the work as a whole first. Then I compose the details. In working out, I always lose something. This cannot be avoided. There is always some loss when we materialize. But there is a compensating gain in vitality. We all have technical difficulties which arise, not from inability to handle the material, but from some inherent quality in the idea. And it is this idea, this first thought, that must dictate the structure and the texture of the work.

RODRIGUEZ: This brings us somewhat close to biology and theology. You bring to my mind the first words of St. John's gospel ''In the beginning was the Word.''

SCHOENBERG: Of course. What else? What else can I do than to express the original Word, which to me is a human thought, a human idea or a human aspiration? Only that I am always doing it better. More clearly, more distinctly, with better language. In other words, my technique adapts itself better to my ideas. But what is this about biology?

RODRIGUEZ: Merely this: that functions preceded organs, or better still, that the necessity of a function created the form and nature of the organ. I am evolutionist enough to believe that running was first a necessity before legs came into being; not that we first had a liver and then were we given a circulatory system to give the liver a job.

SCHOENBERG: This makes me think of my new

**148**

violin concerto. I believe that in it I have created the necessity for a new kind of violinist.

RODRIGUEZ: I have heard something about this. A virtuoso recently told me that the concerto is unplayable until violinists can grow a new fourth finger especially adapted to play on the same string at the same stop as three other fingers.

SCHOENBERG: (laughing like a pleased child): Yes, yes. That will be fine. The concerto is extremely difficult, just as much for the head as for the hands. I am delighted to add another *unplayable* work to the repertoire. I want the concerto to be difficult and I want the little finger to become longer. I can wait.

RODRIGUEZ: Hanslick once advised pianists to have a surgeon at hand when they practised the Chopin studies.

SCHOENBERG: Marvelous! We spoke of a recent concert during which a fine virtuoso chose for his local debut the Mendelssohn concerto. I deplored the choice, subscribing to the vogue of considering Mendelssohn banal, and more important, wishing that new players gave some opportunity to new works.

**149**

SCHOENBERG: You are wrong, my dear. Mendelssohn is a very great master. Brahms said he was the last great master. The trouble is that they always play him too sentimentally. (He imitated the exaggerated manner so common with young ladies of delivering the first theme). Some musicians are underrated; Mahler, for instance. I consider him very great. He also will have his day.

Later on, Otto Klemperer independently said the same thing. He had been deeply touched by the concerto's performance, which he conducted. Come to think about it, in my secret self I also like it. There are memories. But nevertheless new music must have a hearing.

RODRIGUEZ: One thing puzzled me about this matter of systems. I have never been able to detect the fundamental difference between counterpoint and harmony. When I write harmony, I lead the voices contrapuntally; when I write counterpoint I unconsciously keep in mind the harmonic intimations.

SCHOENBERG: You are not the only one. The difference is much deeper. I might put it this way: Harmony,

**150**

as a study, is an extract of musical facts arranged in a theoretical way for pedagogic purposes. Counterpoint is also a teaching method, but one that should prepare for contrapuntal composition. Counterpoint is a way of composing. So when a pupil masters it, he has composed—not learned theory.

RODRIGUEZ: (sighing). One of my greatest regrets is that I composed long before I knew the difference between an interval and a chord. Now I am painfully wrestling with matters that should by this time have been second-nature to me.

SCHOENBERG: Who hasn't? Achron composed important works before he studied, a string quartet, a sonata, and so forth. I have also done the same thing. To my mind, creative and analytical work should go hand in hand, simultaneously.

RODRIGUEZ: Is it possible, dear master, that you are reversing the most hateful of all proverbs, most hateful because most false: "Look before you leap?"

SCHOENBERG: We learn best by doing, if that is what you mean. Theory becomes more significant, more

**151**

applicable and more understandable when we discover its principles after having struggled with the problem.

RODRIGUEZ: Very well, then; I can think of a number of jumps that should be taken.

SCHOENBERG: So? (With gentle malice).

RODRIGUEZ: Hmn. Now here's something that has irritated me a little. Some one, I forget who, at least he is a musician of some note, told me that it was not possible to have form without tonality. And, after reading your Harmonielehre it seemed to me that you had refuted the statement before it was made.

SCHOENBERG: Yes, I think so. And I have also written something about it for Armitage's book. So do not let us repeat.

●

At this moment, I do not know what Schoenberg has written for Armitage's book. But I have some ideas that may not duplicate the master's clarification and I present them thus:

In all music, not only Schoenberg's, no structural system can be said to contain in it the germ or the body of

**152**

form. Techniques are formed by principles, just as organs are formed by functions. Any study of Schoenberg's scores will demonstrate this, for Schoenberg's technique is notably an outgrowth of his musical thought and is molded, altered and developed by the pressure of the idea, just as the skull accommodates itself to the shape of the brain.

Now, to consider this technique as an element that co-operates toward the establishment of form is one thing; to consider it as the *sine qua non* of form is stuff and nonsense. The question is not new. The world is full of works that are merely specimens of a technique that was first painfully evolved and perfected to meet a certain specific requirement of expression. The easiest thing in the world is to mimic technical methods. Any young writer can produce passages in the manner of Carlyle, Proust, Sterne or Cabell, to name the most obviously mannered; students of painting can without great trouble put on canvas a torso that would pass, except to the knowing eye, for fragments of Velazquez or Titian; it is child's play for a musician to write pieces so closely resembling Schumann, Debussy or Franck that only complete knowledge of these masters' repertoire would detect the fraud. In other words, the technical medium, in this case tonality, grew out of a feeling for expression — best called musical thought — that evolved its own body as it was needed. Any one can ape technique; to create form is quite another thing.

There are always a number of musicians dedicated to the fallacy that if one only knows enough harmony, counterpoint or other constructional methods, one cannot fail to erect musical edifices of solid, permanent and logical proportions. They feel that harmony is the first step, very much as if architects restricted their training to growing oak trees and baking bricks.

The reader who is equipped to understand the difficult problems that arise from a serious discussion of tonality —did you every try to define tonality?—will find much information in the work by Stein mentioned above, when he comes to delve into the question of the Schoenbergian system of twelve-notes. I will merely say that to me, this system only amounts to an increase in the available notes of the conventional major or minor modes, with, of course, the consequent elaborations of the resultant harmonies. With the diatonic scales we have also basic patterns, like the Schoenbergian *grundgestalt;* themes, in other words, of changed or only modified shapes which are inverted or reversed. In both systems the patterns or themes may be handled freely, except that Schoenberg, dispensing with tonality, is not fettered to the Procrustean bed of dominant and sub-dominant relationships and the rest of the orthodox harmonic statutes.

Now back to Schoenberg's fireside.

SCHOENBERG: I am somewhat sad that people talk so much of atonality, of twelve-tone systems, of technical methods when it comes to my music. All music, all human work, has a skeleton, a circulatory and nervous system. I wish that my music should be considered as an honest and intelligent person who comes to us saying something he feels deeply and which is of significance to all of us.

RODRIGUEZ: And who, to many of us, is a beautiful and disturbing person; beautiful because disturbing, disturbing because beautiful.

And this is precisely why I venture to predict Schoenberg's music will make its way in the world, against fear, against opposition, against misunderstanding. It is based on eternal principles, it has no patience with the quick, easy and superficial victory, it bears the stamp of a great heart and a great mind. It has to be heard often, studied closely, seen with clear eyes and heard with quickened ears. Then we detect in its voice the moving and radiant timbre of truth. And that is all, my dear friends, that makes a work of art a divinely necessary thing in this enchanting world of ours.

[1937]

156

# C A R L   E N G E L

When the Nazis, wielding the blind broom of racial prejudice, swept out of Germany, along with less desirable elements, the Jewish flower of art and science, they lost their last authentic composer of the German Romantic School, the "modernist" Arnold Schoenberg. Though born, like Fuehrer Hitler, an Austrian, Schoenberg, like the amazing Adolf, is at heart more Teuton than was Hermann, chief of the Cherusci. His dialect may betray the native of the old *Kaiserstadt* on the banks of the Danube; but his musical speech—as his best prose writing—represents, consequentially developed, the sum total of German logic, German rigor, and, unavoidably, German sentiment. His banishment, therefore, is a piece of the grimmest irony.

The sentimental quality of Schoenberg's "modernistic" music links it to that of the Romantics; the logic and rigor of his craftsmanship form his bond with the Classics. If Beethoven begat Brahms, and Richard

**157**

Wagner begat Richard Strauss, Brahms and Strauss begat Arnold Schoenberg. In Beethoven's throbbing adagios and Wagner's soaring cantilenas there pulses as much *Gefühl* as lurks in Brahm's homely folk-themes and in Strauss's rather cloying *Liedertafel* sixths and thirds of which he was never able to rid himself.

Of lesser stature than Beethoven and Wagner, Arnold Schoenberg is more "original" than either Brahms or Strauss. He has sought a path of his own and found it. It is not a road for the many to travel. Some that have tried to follow his lead have perished in the quicksands of musical aridity. Perhaps precisely because they lacked the quickening and humanizing grace of Schoenberg's "Sentiment." Of his disciples only Alban Berg came up to the master; and possibly a later day may find it difficult to decide which of the two surpassed the other. Berg died at an age when, presumably, he still had his best to give to the world.

In a recent book on the "process of musical creation," the German author of it quotes some interesting statements of Schoenberg's regarding his "style-develop-

**158**

ment.'' Schoenberg tells us that he ''was driven forward by a desire for conciseness, precision, sharpness, and distinctiveness.'' If not absolute synonyms, these terms partake of the same hue. And the exact shade that Schoenberg tried to find was a musical expression at once better, clearer, less ambiguous, and more personal. That Schoenberg's ''personality'' or his musical profile has consistently increased in sharpness as his style and his art have evolved, no one will deny. But it does not seem that time has altered in any way the inborn and inalienable traits that stamp him the legitimate off-spring of his great German elders. He did not pull up his roots, he let them sink deeper.

The last of the ''three times seven'' poems that constitute Schoenberg's ''Pierrot Lunaire'' begins significantly with the line ''O alter Duft aus Märchenzeit.'' And this ancient aroma, this lingering scent not only pervades long stretches of the ''Gurrelieder'' as well as the settings to the Germanized verses of the Belgian Kaeyenberg who, under the name of Albert Giraud, wrote French *rondeaux* about the eternal and universal Emotionalist,

**159**

but it can be found—here and there, in smaller or larger doses—in practically everything that Schoenberg has composed. And, to be sure, it is one of the most unmistakably German characteristics of his music.

Schoenberg frankly helped himself to the "alter Duft" when lately he turned to Handel and Monn for his *materia musica* and when he wrote a suite for string orchestra "in the olden style." His is not, we believe, a case of being at his wits' end in the quest for "something new"—as it would seem to be with the neo-classicism and pseudo-romanticism of Stravinsky's later phases,—but an atavistic streak and a decidedly German idiosyncrasy to reach out for the "alter Duft" as Beethoven did in writing variations on themes whose perfume sometimes was a little faded (even in his day), as Wagner did in "Die Meistersinger," as Brahms did in the Handel and Paganini variations (Schumann and Liszt also succumbed to Nicolo's volatile fragrance and tried to give it "body"), and as Strauss did in the music for "Le Bourgeois Gentilhomme" and in certain parts of "Der Rosenkavalier." None of them could quite forget the "alter Duft," strive as they might, and "progressive" as each may have been in his way.

An astute English critic, some years ago, after hearing Schoenberg's "Pierrot Lunaire" confessed that the quality of the work that impressed him chiefly was its "Teutonic *Herzlichkeit*." Now, this heartiness is perhaps even more an Austrian characteristic than it is Teuton. And anyone having had the privilege of knowing Schoenberg intimately will agree that there is no one more "herzlich" or cordial than he. But in music this quality can result in only one thing: "from the heart it comes, to the heart it should go."

Schoenberg's music has been decried by many as that of a mere theorist, of a juggler with dry and lifeless formulae; few have accorded it "sentiment," or have accepted its "sentimentality." Old Doctor Burney quaintly but shrewdly observed that "it is somewhat remarkable, that from all the learned and operose calculations of professed mathematicians, not a single piece of practical music has ever been produced, that is supportable to the ear of persons of taste; so true it is, that the operations of cool and deliberate reflection have less power over our feelings than those of passion and enthusiasm." The passion and enthusiasm in much of Schoenberg's music are not of the ordinary kind, but they are there nevertheless and most obviously when they take the form of "Teutonic *Herzlichkeit*." Thomas Carlyle, the most Germanic of British minds, declared that "the barrenest of all mortals is the sentimentalist." That is but a grouchy *boutade*. Sentimentality need not be shallow, sentiment need not be mawkish. But without "the softer emotions" being stirred in us, art can not really move us. And whenever Schoenberg's music is the most deeply moving, its German logic and rigor are tinged and softened with German sentiment, which comes closer to being sentimentality.

Perhaps Schoenberg's greatest achievement consists in having extracted from the old ingredients a new flavor, a fresh bouquet: that "personal" note for which in his "style-development" he has so persistently striven. He has filled our nostrils with the breath of a new dawn, roseate, not with old, but with sempiternal warmth that springs, not from the head, but from the heart. He has reminded us, or taught us anew, that the great composers of tomorrow, no less than did those of yesterday, will have to leave a little room for "sentiment," if they wish their music to outlive today.

Was it not Victor Hugo who acclaimed Baudelaire's "Flowers of Evil" by admitting that these poems had at last given him "un nouveau frisson," a new shiver down his back? Well, the merit of any piece of music, as of poetry, is ultimately measured by the number of shivers it sends down a sensitive listener's back. And those shivers are not produced by any "operose calculations" of the brain, but by spontaneous outbursts of sentiment, infinitely and indeterminately renewed. *O neuer Duft!*

[1937]

163

# BERTHOLD VIERTEL

## I

The text of "Die Jakobsleiter" was published years ago; the composer has not yet finished the music.

The words, without the music, show the great plan of the oratorio, the architecture of cathedral proportion. The text is a creation in language, expressing the theme and its variations, developing the thought in the most precise form. There exists no translation. So, when I refer to the book in the following remarks, it is like describing adventures in a strange country into which English speaking people can not enter. It is hard to describe such a mental world, foreign in this respect, too, that its vegetation takes new forms, never seen before; that its creator has a mind of his own, a truly original mind.

One might answer that it must be easier to give the meaning of words than of music. What is written, can be rationally examined, while the hearer of music who de-

**165**

nies that the sounds he hears make sense to him, could ultimately be referred only to sheer mathematics( symbols without feeling) : words, even the most difficult ones, should offer the possibility of translation into a simpler, common language. Most people are ready to believe so. But the Shakespearean diction, for example, can not be reduced to a précis, a mere statement of the sense, without losing its true meaning. Poetic diction is the most exact expression of a thought. You can not strip Shakespeare of verse and rhythm, you can not explain his imagery without robbing the creator's action of its vital purpose. The productive act, in its real significance is an attack on our receptivity which no paraphrase can replace and which can not be watered down and made more palatable. The creator himself had to concentrate all his power in order to reach the heights which we have to climb afterwards with his help, with his form as only guide.

Diction, in this severe sense, is the text of "Die Jakobsleiter."

## II

Mention of Shakespearean diction reminds us that

Schoenberg's text is poetry. It is not quite that, but something of the same sort. I would define it as a mental process in which language is not the garment, but the body of the thought, its physiognomy changing with every word.

Schoenberg could not write and talk differently. His mind seems to be of the kind that attacks every problem at the root. This mind of his is surely not without a tradition. But whatever he found on his way, already existing and obliging him by its existence, he had to examine thoroughly.

It is Schoenberg's very nature, to deal with essentials. Not that his mind is utterly "abstract." It is a philosophic mind.

It may be objected that philosophy is not the business of an artist. By what we call "art" is generally meant "play"; a kind of play that never arrives at a clear and conscious mental system. The "eternal child" is supposed to be more alive in an artist than in the rest of us. This opinion has developed so far that there exists in the public's mind an equation between "art" and "entertainment." And "thinking" offers entertainment only to a very restricted minority. It is necessary, therefore, to be reminded of the fact that Schoenberg is a great artist before I dare to call him a thinker. He is a man of imagination, primarily; he plays, masterfully, with sounds. Before everything else, he is a musician, a composer. And as such inventive in the highest degree; obstinately so. He wants to play with his own sounds in his own way. But—he wants his sounds to express his thoughts, as he can not help thinking his own thoughts. His music is the language of his heart, but an essential part of his heart is his brain.

May I, a layman, dare to make a remark about Schoenberg's music? If, following Schopenhauer's definition, Richard Wagner's music is the direct language of the "will" (will-being the general, all-embracing idea of all forces driving within us), then I would define Schoenberg's music as being much more the language of distinct "volition." By this I do not wish to indicate a limitation. Of course, all the unconsciously driving forces within, feed Schoenberg's music, as well as Wagner's.

**168**

The conquest an artist makes in the realm of the subconscious provides him with a great part of his material. Like every original artist, Schoenberg illuminates hitherto un-guessed-at inner darknesses with the strong light of consciousness. But, it seems to me that in spite of the delicacy of the fine spun nervous web, the muscular system, the distinct purpose of the volition, is developed in Schoenberg to a Spartan-like virility. His central problem is an ethical one. His sensuality is rich, but chaste; the leadership of the mind is gloriously established in his work. In spite of the extreme modernism, the main attitude is a classical one, a pious one, one might say: a religious one. The questioning of the meaning and aim of life is always urgent, as struggle, doubt, longing, as a dramatic and powerful impulse. From darkness to light, from chaos to cosmos by mastery of form, Schoenberg points out one road, but it is the road of his heroic experience, never a compromise with a stifled conscience, with an easy solution, with some nirvana, with any convention or any cheap optimism. His admission of disharmony, his renunciation of repetition—acknowl-

**169**

edging only necessity as a criterion—has, quite obviously, an ethical meaning.

These are characteristics of Schoenberg's attitude. Superficial critics might call the inventor of the method of composition with twelve tones a reformer by nature— a complete misapprehension. Schoenberg always thrusts through the fundamentals with irrevocable definitiveness. The word "reformer" is not radical enough: it utterly fails to describe his behaviour. It would be even better to say that his primary endeavor is to turn things upside down.

His mind is paradoxical. The paradox belongs to the impulse which makes him play. It provides a method, which is often very thrilling but never carries him away. It is not Schoenberg's aim to be paradoxical or refined; nor is it either the old style, or the new, merely for the sake of its newness. The aim is: to become a legislator.

### III

A law-maker. It is not only music that receives new laws from him. "Die Jakobsleiter" looks like the catechism of a new religion. Of Schoenberg's religion.

I am afraid to touch upon the religious question. Schoenberg isn't. His fundamentalism is not afraid of its most daring consequences.

Before he writes an oratorio, he asks himself: what is, truly, a prayer? The choral works of Johan Sebastian Bach were founded, religiously, not only in the soul of a believer, but, by uninterrupted tradition, in an official creed, they were in complete unanimity with an existing church, with Protestantism. Schoenberg is a free thinker. At the cradle of his mentality stands doubt, the most universal doubt. As a modern man, at the end of the nineteenth, the beginning of the twentieth century, he has witnessed and studied the all conquering victory of science. He is of his age, the age of extreme individualism. Wasn't the principal, "l'art pour l'art" an outcome of this time and age? But form—as an aim in itself—gives no satisfying solution to a mind like Schoenberg's. Form, after all, is empty, if it fails to form something of vital importance.

Schoenberg could not write an oratorio merely because it is beautiful to pray. He asks immediately: "Do we

pray?—Who does?—When?—Why do we pray?—What
is the root of praying?—Its aim?—Its effect?'' Praying
becomes a fundamental problem to him. And not only
his individual problem—but a general one. The problem
of humanity. He must understand it universally, as action and fulfillment of the human soul—and in all its
possibilities. He thinks it through in all its forms. He
may have done so for years. Until, one day, the religious
thinker, Schoenberg, had a vision which became the inspiration of the artist.

### IV

The vision of ''Die Jakobsleiter'' reaches back to the
Old Testament. ''And Jacob went out from Beer-sheba,
and went toward Haran. And he lighted upon a certain
place and tarried there all night, because the sun was
set; and he took of the stones of that place, and put them
for his pillows, and lay down in that place to sleep. And
he dreamed, and behold a ladder set up on the earth, and
the top of it reached to heaven: and behold the angels of
God ascending and descending on it. And behold the
Lord stood above it—''

**172**

It is not the following promise of the Lord that awakened Schoenberg's vision. It is the upward movement between earth and heaven, the ladder, on which the angels ascend and descend: leading the human soul, the soul of man who prays. The prayer creates the connection with God on the top of the ladder, above it. There is a quotation from Balzac's "Seraphita" in the oratorio: "Who prays has become one with God." And a choir sings from the highest point of the ladder: "Union with Him awakes magnetically the currents of the mind by induction—" giving an ultra modern interpretation of the same phenomenon.

The religious aspect is neither Jewish nor Christian, even if the action of the oratorio has a certain relation to the liturgy. All kind of theoretical, merely philosophical solutions are dealt with; the scholar will find a thorough richness of allusion and will admire how all is interwoven in the tense dialectical development expressing a powerful effort toward fulfillment—the last and highest solution of all the disparate human errors and aspirations, the unification of the innumerable tendencies upwards that create the dramatic movement in one direction. This vision, as such, is fit for music, for a main theme and its variations, for a contrapuntal development between the obstacles and the gradual achievement, for a complicated series of disharmonies, ultimately fused in harmony—the union of the disparate.

<h2 style="text-align:center">V</h2>

The cosmogony that Schoenberg unfolds in this work is of amazing dimensions. A landscape of the soul, like a fissured, mountainous region where, in characteristic positions, all kinds of human beings are distributed in various stages of development, all on the way upwards; upwards, step by step, a swarming caravan of endeavour. Each experience in life, love and work means, as the road rises, a relative peak, or lowland; every achievement is discredited because it opens up a new problem and shows a fresh summit to conquer. When the drama begins, they are already wandering about in a fluent movement forward, upward: dissatisfied people; doubters; triumphant ones; fighters; rebels; some disheartened and giving up, giving in; others on the unending search; lovers of beauty; lovers of love; some who have found, only to lose again; he who struggles; he who is chosen—and he who is appointed. All desires and purposes seem to be on the move, every form of will and volition in the earthly zone. They are tired, they strive on, as time drives them, time being the actuality of our urge and the potentiality of imperfection. They do not know whither the journey leads. Gabriel is among them, the archangel, giving help and advice, judging them, leading them on—where to? Onwards, upwards.

Then, an incision: death, death in the middle of the way. Death who interrupts everyone, the climber as well as the indolent; the dying man is a solo, because every dying man is alone. Wonderful and untouchably tender is this transformation of death, with an unheard of simplicity. The work of a poet. The soul sees its most blessed dream coming true: "I am flying—" The soul transgresses with a drawn out "Oh - - - - " which sounds half painful and half joyously astonished.

An orchestral intermezzo of some length follows.

Then, simultaneously with the broad singing of Gabriel,

**175**

voices of women from far ahead. And while the soul is singing in drawn out tones without words, a group of voices, men and women, begin to be heard: we have entered, together with the soul of the dying man, the realm of the souls, after death. And there again: the same continuous movement upwards, continuing as if death were no boundary.

As in the visions of Swedenborg, life after death is revealed as the direct continuation of all striving and erring, the climbing up the "gradus ad parnassum" toward completion and fulfillment. Demons, genii, stars, Gods and angels, we meet as we go on. They are the complements of all earthly types, helping them to their higher possibilities, giving definitions and offering solutions. "Die Jakobsleiter" reaches up and down, an infinite way, that may be taken endlessly in both directions. And, while this proceeds, while some of the souls prepare themselves for higher climbing, others for return into human form and life in order to repeat the task, we become with them aware of the directing and unifying magic that is in the prayer, which gives the striving wings, spends consolation and admonition, contains self-sacrifice, enables inner change and re-birth. Every gesture of the soul will be directed by prayer, helping the unending process which penetrates matter with mind, burning as a purifying flame, till no cinders are left, and the ultimate harmony is reached. That is the miracle expressed in "Die Jakobsleiter." Voices gather into groups. Choirs from the depths are answered by choirs from the heights: the main choir announces the great motive of the oratorio, and prayer streams into harmony.

## VI

To make death not the end but the counterpoint of life: in that lies the greatness of this conception. By this, Schoenberg, the thinker, reveals himself as a mystic. Or, simply, as a religious man, expressing his definite faith in salvation through the spirit. It is as an artist that he visualizes the form this procedure takes. He creates the world of the living as a pilgrimage toward solution, distinct in every form and thought. The types of human behaviour are, each of them, originally characterized, judged and interpreted, in relation to their goal, by a

177

moralist who measures hope and despair, failure and success by his own deep experiences, never merely condemning, but always aware of the upward tendencies, supporting, advising, teaching. To go into the details of the life philosophy behind all this, means study. A study that offers rich results.

In Schoenberg's moralizing there is so much common sense, so practical an ability to deal with the inefficiencies and discrepancies of human nature in order to turn them into productive fruitfulness. It is the creed of an artist, for whom achievement and happiness, everything in life that seems definite, is only the spur to further Faustian endeavor. The spirit of the work is unlimited courage, and, in this respect, unconquerable optimism.

The form reaches from the most exact definitions, the sharpest aphorisms, to the sighs and stammerings of the simple soul. Such as the "gently resigned" ones (die sanft Ergebenen—: (a bit childish, very monotonous):

"—so one takes it as it comes—"
(becoming steadily softer, tempo slower and slower)
"yes, yes  .  .  .  .

**178**

yes, yes  .  .  .  .

.  .  .  .  .  .  .  .

yes, yes  .  .  .  as it comes,

it comes  .  .  .  .

yes, yes  .  .  .  .

one takes it  .  .  .

and bears it  .  .

.  .  .  .  .  .  .  .  .

as it comes  .  .  .

.  .  .  .  .  .  .  .

yes  .  .  .  .  .  .

(in spite of the pp the whole choir gradually joins in, so
that the end is being sung by all)

yes  .  .  .  .

as it comes  .  .

Immediately follows a choir—:

(very lyrically, beautifully sung):

"O  .  .  .  .  .  .

how beautiful it is to live in the mud  .  .

yes  .  .  .

.  .  .  .  .

**179**

```
yes  .  .  .  .  .

yes  .  .  .  .  yes.''
```

This example may have a popular appeal by its whimsically tragic humor which does not shrink from apparent banalities. It illustrates, too, what I called the paradoxical trait in Schoenberg's mind. And it shows how concrete his vision is, how close to life, how experienced.

But it does not give any indication of the great sermons and choral passages in which the most difficult thoughts are enunciated with the same distinctiveness as are mere impulses, in the above example.

I do not doubt that the music will give the abstract words an underlying emotional colour, will make them—as well as the whole dramatic action—lucid and transparent, understandable even to the listener who misses the meaning of the words.

On the other hand, to understand this music—and all music of Schoenberg—this concentrated formulation of his life philosophy offers to the reader the greatest help. It shows the inner drama, expressed both, in his music and in his thought, aphoristic in detail and streaming in a mighty flow in its continuity, over the widest span of disharmony to the last fulfilling chord, reaching the goal of the artist as well as that of the fighter, the seeker, and the man.

[1937]

**181**

# OTTO KLEMPERER

When I heard Schoenberg's first Quartett performed in January, 1937, at the Schoenberg Festival in U. C. L. A. my thoughts wandered back thirty years: it was in Dresden in 1907 during the annual festival of the "Allgemeine Deutsche Musikverein." We listened to Schoenberg's first Quartett for the first time in Germany. It was an extraordinary event, friends and enemies of that great composer could be recognized immediately and clearly. I don't believe, that today there is any opposition left against this rich and warm first Quartett, of which the essence is today as strong as in 1907. Five years later in 1912 Schoenberg performed for the first time his "Pierrot Lunaire" in Hamburg. What an amazing score! An orchestra of five musicians. Sounds appeared, which never were heard before. Sometimes it sounded like an orchestra of 100 men. And again there appeared strong and forceful admirers on the one side and hard-headed opponents on the other. Then we

**183**

entered the world war and the post war period, which opened the doors for all those, who were scorned and boycotted under the old regime. Schoenberg was now "en vogue." The first concert I personally conducted in Berlin in 1920 was devoted to two early Schoenberg works. "Verklaerte Nacht" and "Pelleas." No more opposition. An unified enthusiastic audience! When I had the honor to make the first performance of "Pierrot" (1922 in Cologne) the success was so strong, that we had to repeat the last two poems. Time went on and the reactionary powers of old became stronger and stronger in Germany. Schoenberg was now in Berlin as Professor on the Akademie for Composition, (the most highly honored position Germany had to offer). But the permanent fight with all the reactionary elements made it difficult to work for Schoenberg at that time. Our group (around the Kroll-Opera) tried to promote Schoenberg's music, but we could not do all we wanted. We performed his two operas "Erwartung" and "Glueckliche Hand." Especially "Erwartung" a Monodrama, expressing the feeling of a loving woman betrayed by her lover, is another very strong Schoenberg work, which perhaps like no other of the works of Schoenberg expresses the most delicate human feelings. This was in 1930. Who could dream, that five years later we would meet in California? Now Los Angeles can be proud and happy to possess Arnold Schoenberg, as leader of the Music Department at U. C. L. A. For he is not only a creative genius, he is the greatest living teacher as well. His work—naturally—is being discussed even nowadays. And there is no doubt, that it is difficult to follow Schoenberg, especially in his last twelve-tone period. But have we the right to criticize these works written in a new musical language? Let us at first learn this language. However the personal reaction may be, one thing is certain: Schoenberg never wrote a single note which was not justified in itself, he wandered his paths from his very beginnings unmoved by the fashions of the day. He never cared for Impressionism nor for Expressionism, neither for Neoclassicism nor for Surrealism, he cared for music. I would call him the *composer of the extraordinary,* because there is not one score of his pen, which would not appear as an extraordinary achievement. Whether you listen to his "Verklaerte Nacht" or to his "Gurrelieder," whether you listen to his "Chambersinfonie" or his last fourth Quartett, each and every work has a very different type of its own, but everyone of them carries the impress of an extraordinary genius.

[1936]

**186**

# PAUL AMADEUS PISK

When so creative a spirit as Arnold Schönberg turns to the music theatre, we can expect that he will write not ordinary operas, light operas or *Gebrauchsmusik,* but works of art introducing to the drama those problems in absolute music that he solved for the whole world years ago. Even his first two works for the stage, the monodrama, *Die Erwartung,* and *Die Glückliche Hand,* were musical delineations of spiritual experiences materialized by the medium of the stage. There too, the artistic effect was achieved by purely musical means, the dramatic content contributing its color with unusual restraint.

These two early works were completed before Schönberg had perfected the twelve-tone technic which he has since utilized with increasing freedom as the basis of his work in pure music. The fundamental principles of this technic may be briefly recalled. Just as the logical relation between the individual notes of the melody in music of the seven-step scale is revealed by melodic and harmonic cadences, in twelve-tone music it is established by a fixed arrangement of tonal material maintained throughout the course of a composition. Since the basic figure of the twelve-tone series is often repeated, though in a great diversity of forms, the composition achieves a new unity which permits the utmost variation in melodic and rhythmic patterns. For the basic figure of the series is not always the same; it can be inverted, it can appear in a crab (backwards) and in an inversion of the crab. In Schönberg's newest works the series is also transposed, that is, employed in several pitches, and, moreover, divided up among several voices and instruments.

Schönberg's new composition, *Von Heute auf Morgen,* is a gay opera. The composer made a point of demonstrating that the difficult structure of the twelve-tone technic can lend itself to light and cheerful expression. He uses a one-act text by Max Blonda which takes about fifty minutes to present. The plot is in a modern setting and it is necessary to follow it closely, for the structural form of the music arises directly out of the scene sequence and is also closely related to the dramatic characterization. A young couple return home after a social evening. The man grows enthusiastic about his wife's friend, a clever woman with great sex appeal, compared to whom his simple, loyal spouse seems pale. The wife realizes her husband's state of mind, and forms a dangerous plan to cure him. A harmless affair with a stupid tenor serves her purpose. She changes her appearance and behavior to conform to the worldly ideal of her husband. When he is again enamored she reveals the perils of this mode of life. She must have noisy entertainment, wine, dancing; she neglects her child, slights domestic duties and leads her husband to believe that the singer is her lover. The man has a spiritual revelation and gains a better sense of values. The nocturnal "intermezzo" closes with a return to reality of the ending. The puppets of today are motivated by a second pair who appear upon the scene, the wife's friend and the singer, who seem to lead lives of their own, but are in reality only shadowy figures of the theatre. But—ironic paradox—for them their lives are the reality, the lives of the other pair the dream. A quartet based on the interaction of these four

characters is the climax of the opera, to which a short
lyric coda is added, where, as in *Pierrot Lunaire,* the
chanted, spoken word is used instead of singing, to ac-
centuate the actuality and reality. But the play is not yet
ended. By way of contrast to the fashion, real people are
made by love. The external world changes from one day
to another. Hence the question with which the child ends
the piece: ''What are these objects, modern men?''

The dramatist Schönberg is able, as was Mozart on a
different plane, to characterize these four figures *entirely
in terms of melody.* The tone of the singer is somewhat
lyric, artificially sweet, a parody of romanticism; that of
the friend affectedly witty; that of the wife now sharp,
now warm, flowing on naturally. These melodic themes
are not only fixed in the intervals of the twelve-tone
technic, but they also display a marked rhythmic structure, so characteristic indeed that certain parts of the
series are made to recur as unmistakable rythmic motifs.
Thus the singer is identified not only by a broad and
flowing melody in six-quarter time, but also by occasional
recurring suggestions of dance rhythms, easily recogniz-

able as the waltz or the tango. Furthermore, in the melodies there is contrapuntal development, as in the interchanges in the duet through double counterpoint or canons in various leadings. Double canons also, and very skillful interweavings appear on close study.

In the larger formal sense the opera is constructed of distinct parts and recitatives. Recitatives are indicated as such and easily recognized. Arias are either strict or are in free arioso form, as, for example, the first, whose important melodic motif reappears later in four places in the opera, though greatly varied and intensified as well as in ever increasing rhythmic complexity. One notes a purely thematic connection between the separate numbers. When the wife speaks of the singer for the first time, and imitates him, she already forecasts the entire musical material of the telephone scene, which is later built up in a different form from the same elements. The enclosed arias of the husband emerge in clear relief. Even a song stanza with a definite, clearly developed counter-strophe appears in this music. It is interesting to note that the rhythm and the inner movement of the arias change with the characteristics of the form. They are intensified to indicate the wife's emotion and remain fairly even during the two arias of the husband. In the very first duet we get a fused portrayal of both characters. It is lively in tone, capricious, to a certain extent flirtatious. Then the expression rapidly changes; the duet of the quarrel is pointed and sharp. Here also one finds a clearly developed canon in the inversion of both voices. The pathos of emotion is grotesquely delineated and further emphasized by the instrumentation. A short orchestral interlude leads to the second aria of the husband, the one worked out in strophes; this evolves into a free arioso. In the following buffo-scene a construction new to opera is attempted; in the closed phrase a series of motifs is introduced, constructed one above the other and containing all the thematic material out of which the following scenes are composed. The telephone scene, which, as I have said, is made up of earlier motifs in a new form, has a very easily defined structure. There are two strophes, a middle part, and a coda. Noteworthy here is the mawkish lyrical character contrasting so sharply with the preceding passage and also with the episode of the child's entrance so delicately orchestrated with solo instruments. An orchestral interlude at the climax leads into the conclusion, at the same time indicating a change in the character of the music from the forced to the real. The quartet combines these two melodic characteristics.

Even those in the audience who cannot follow the technic of Schönberg's music will be carried away by its expressive power, materially aided as they are by the orchestration. The orchestra is average in size. There are saxophones, mandolins and guitars, which often appear in solo parts, the piano, and the flexaton. The instruments are combined with greatest freedom. Solo strings, often contra-bass and cello, play in combination with wind instruments, at times with the transparent quality of a chamber symphony, at others in the fullest sonority. Schönberg also resorts to humorous, clever tone painting. Solo violins, saxophones, and piccolo trills create a champagne-like effervescence, while low string instruments and percussion, in conjunction with the deep saxophone, portray the dullness of a person walking witlessly into a trap, or a child receiving school discipline. Hovering above the strict formal unity there is a fantastic and free tonal play. The combination of these two elements outstandingly accounts for the charm of the piece.

[1930]

194

# P A U L   S T E F A N

We shall consider here, three stage works by Arnold Schoenberg, two of them written rather early in his career; the third being a comparatively recent work. Between the appearance of the two earlier operas and the completion of this third one there is an interval of fifteen years, during which time Schoenberg has moved along a road which it is not yet possible to map out very clearly. The two earlier works reveal a Schoenberg vastly different from the master of these latter years.

Let us recall a few significant dates here. In 1924 his native city, Vienna, having long ignored him after greeting his first concert with jeers and laughter, at last feted her composer with exaggerated zeal. He was invited to the City Hall; the mayor warmly saluted him and in the presence of the assembled guests proclaimed him a leader of his generation. The chorus of the State Opera House then sang Schoenberg's *Friede auf Erden,* a work up to then considered almost impossible to perform. This did

**195**

not prevent Schoenberg from leaving Vienna three years later (as he had left it so often before) to go to Berlin, for there only, and not at home, he found a suitable sphere and a sympathetic environment. The Prussian Ministry of Arts and Sciences had appointed him instructor in composition at the Berlin Academy of Arts. He was required to live in Berlin only six months of the year, and had ample leisure for creative work. Such a position and such a salary were not to be had in Vienna.

The celebration of Schoenberg's fiftieth birthday coincided approximately with the end of a period of crisis in the composer's artistic development. During this time, as a result of theoretical investigation, he had arrived at the doctrine of his twelve-tone system. With this as a basis he again turned to composition and completed, in quick succession, the series of works which begins with Opus 23 for piano. He still regards this theory as perfectly valid, and his own immediate pupils adhere to it. Such masterpieces as Schoenberg's *Third Quartet,* Anton Berg's *Lyrical Suite,* and the *String Trio* of Anton von Webern were all composed in strict accordance with

Schoenberg's rules. Theory alone, however, is evidently insufficient, for works have already appeared which adhere scrupulously enough to the rules but do not reveal a genius such as that of the composers named above.

Schoenberg needed new tools, new bearings, a new mold. He had written a wonderful treatise on harmony, one of the most brilliant books ever penned on music and on art in general, in which he treats the sacrosanct laws of the old school as nothing more than rules of thumb. These he examines and interprets for the reader, indicating their *raison d'etre* as he goes. Only in the concluding chapter is one forwarned that new rules must come, that a new art has arisen. One of the first prophets of this new art and one of its mightiest personalities, has been Schoenberg himself.

Schoenberg was not and is not a professional revolutionary. In the oratorio, *Die Jakobsleiter,* an uncompleted work of his middle period, he reveals himself unmistakably a martyr of the new era, a man driven against his will to wrestle with the angels, to take upon himself the proclamation of the New. Had he chosen to remain upon the broad beaten highway, he would have found ease and have won early recognition. For after a difficult youth in Vienna and in Berlin, he experienced several triumphs, one even on the occasion of the first presentation of his great choral work, *Die Gurre-Lieder,* in Vienna in 1913. And *Pierrot Lunaire,* a work markedly different from *Die Gurre-Lieder,* received enthusiastic applause, despite sharp criticism.

It is only in the light of Schoenberg's almost legendary martyr-life that we can understand how he could complete a work like *Die Gurre-Lieder* at a time when he was wrapped up in the *Pierrot.* For *Die Gurre-Lieder,* although they bring us wholly new spiritual values, although they further integrate Wagner's sonorities, nevertheless issue undeniably from the harmonic world of *Tristan* while with *Pierrot* a state of harmony has been reached which we are accustomed to call atonality. But Schoenberg denies the possibility of atonality. In effect he denies anarchy and insofar as his own compositions are concerned he is wholly right. The succession of his earlier works shows how smoothly and how logically the liberation from harmonies of the seventh and ninth had proceeded, how, further, the pyramiding of chords and the use of suspensions led to the development of harmonic fourths and progressions in fourths. The same powerful logic dominates his rejection of the large form, its dissolution into originally impressionistic tone-pictures, and the reintegration of all the expressive powers of his music in new molds.

During this period of transition, between 1910 and 1920, and soon after the piano pieces, the five orchestral pieces and *Pierrot,* there appeared the two dramatic works, *Erwartung* and *Die Glückliche Hand.* Both *Erwartung* and *Die Glückliche Hand* are to be ranked below the *Pierrot* from the point of view of achieved precision. It is not certain whether Schoenberg at the time actually intended to bring them to the stage. He was living in an almost visionary state. These were the years when, stimulated by Oskar Kokoschka, he also began to paint. His pictures were marvels of logical consistency, powerful in expression and self-revealing; they gave concrete embodiment to certain moods and passages from the symphonies of Gustave Mahler. Everyone who came within range of the man felt his almost miraculous force. His penetration and sensitivity were too keen to be satisfied with the customary modes of expression in music and on the stage. It almost seemed as if Schoenberg had his own premonition of the approaching world catastrophe, was already feeling it in every nerve. Some such prophetic admonition inspires the scenes which succeed one another in his music dramas, the tempo of whose development is as stormy as his own. Both last only a short fraction of an hour. If the short opera is the fashion today, it was Schoenberg who originated it almost two decades ago. *Erwartung* brings a single person on the stage, a woman. In darkest night, in the forest, she comes to a rendezvous with her lover and suddenly she stumbles over his dead body. By intuition she understands that he has known another woman who was the agent of his death. This is Schoenberg's first opera, a "monodrama" set to a poem by Marie Pappenheim. The music is an ecstatic surge of fear and love; it has an eerie splendor.

*Die Glückliche Hand* is leagues beyond this first attempt. It was first presented by Zemlinsky at Prague in 1924, during a festival of The International Society for New Music. Several months later, at the suggestion of the city of Vienna, Dr. Stiedry produced it at the Vienna People's Theatre, where it was twice repeated. The performance proved very costly and the management of the theatre was bitterly criticised. But in 1928 the Opera House at Breslau presented *Die Glückliche Hand* with overwhelming success, without in the least compromising either its schedule or its budget; and again, in 1929, there was a brilliant performance at the Music Festival at Duisburg, where it won such extraordinary acclaim as to compel a repetition after two days.

In *Die Glückliche Hand* action is stripped of all realism; one moves in the sphere of poetry, of symbols, of visions. The scene reveals a Man, astride whose back sits a mythological Beast that will not release him. The chorus chants its sympathy for this victim, who longs for earthly happiness although heavenly joy is his destiny. (This chorus is partly a *Sprech-chor,* speaking in carefully indicated tones, a sort of "melodrama" form al-

**201**

ready introduced by Schoenberg in the *Gurre-Lieder* and in *Pierrot Lunaire*). A Woman, who embodies earthly happiness, deserts the Man for a Stranger, who seems to represent the power of money, as the Man does the power of spirit. For the second time abandoned by the Woman, the Man rises to his full height, and knows, at last, that in controlling his own destiny he possesses the Woman— not in the body, but in the spirit, and so forever. There follows a great battle for golden treasure within a Cave. Once more the Man conquers; but because he dreams of pursuing a new vision of the Woman, he falls finally into the power of the Beast of the first scene. And the chorus mourns: "Must you suffer again what you have so often suffered? Can you make no sacrifice? Can you not be content?"

Through this music we perceive now the lines, now only the colors of a celestial voice. Chords pile upon each other as the lines flow together, eleven and twelve parts simultaneously; the instruments, often in strange, bizarre combination take on an ever increasing role, an extraordinary power and significance. Schoenberg the painter, rounds out the complicated score by exact specifications for unusually rapid shifts of light and colors of symbolic meaning, undoubtedly of the kind anticipated by the light-color music of Scriabin and others.

To comprehend the magnitude of this work it must be heard and seen. There is no doubt that *Die Glückliche Hand* is significant in Schoenberg's development. It marked an inevitable goal, but a goal from which he was forced to depart with equal necessity.

There is another question which might be asked: Does *Die Glückliche Hand* really belong to the body of the new opera as we have seen it develop in the last two or three decades? This cannot be answered off hand. The first two of Schoenberg's dramatic works were too long neglected, stood too long alone. Perhaps they still do. The opera has since traveled along many roads. Let us indicate some of the divergences: *Cardillac* of Hindemith with its action reduced to symbolism; *Oedipus Rex* of Stravinsky, which is so deliberately removed from all dramatic effect, that it even has recourse to a dead tongue; *Jürg Jenatch* of Kaminski, which interweaves song with

**203**

spoken drama; those operas of Krenek (I do not here refer to the *Jonny,* the triumph of whose explicit text is
attested by its great popular success) which rest upon
poetico-symbolic texts; the revue, *Neues vom Tage* of
Hindemith; the three-penny opera, *Schauspiel mit Songs,*
of Kurt Weill—and other works. I believe the composers
of all these works have been acquainted with Arnold
Schoenberg's attempts for the operatic stage; and I also
believe that the whole history of the opera since their appearance shows them to have been of the greatest importance and far-reaching effect.

[1929]

**204**

# FRANZ WERFEL

In Arnold Schönberg's personality and art we honor above all his relentless striving towards the Absolute, a greatness and a strength of will and an ideal of perfection, which is scarcely comprehensable to a purposeless and mindless group of contemporaries. In his wholehearted devotion to this perfection this master of music is most adequately compared to the great masters of the Kabbala. Like these, by "sanctification of The Name," who were intent to draw the divine into the earthly sphere, so Arnold Schönberg endeavors, through the consecration of a work of art, by means of complete elimination of all unclean, secondary motives, to draw the absolute into the world of music. Thus he achieves in the strong and courageous loneliness of the mystic, devoid of approval and sympathy, a work of the highest spiritual conception, for which a more powerfully minded and finer spiritually developed era will be able to find judgment.

[1934]

**205**

# L O U I S   D A N Z

In Nature, laws are merely man's pitiable limitations. How often have we not heard that old-worn cliché "No two leaves are alike." This means simply that we do not know enough leaves. Somewhere at sometime there has been, is, or will be that very leaf whose existence we doubt.

The profound Galileo wrote that Nature is "written in mathematical language." What Galileo said about Nature must also be said about music because music is an indissoluble part of the structure of Nature.

Oswald Spengler with the same clear vision once wrote that "Gothic cathedrals and Doric temples are mathematics in stone." And even stone itself can be called molecular mathematics. Spengler also called attention to the mathematical instinct of the Australian natives. Is not their discovery and use of the boomerang a mathematical symbol of the first order worthy of an Einstein, a Bach—or a Schoenberg, "a sure *feeling* for numbers

**207**

of a class that we should refer to the higher geometry.''

Music is un-conscious mathematics. Psycho-physiologically, music is neural mathematics actualized through sound. The composer does not consciously mathematize but his nerve structures, his neural configurations extend into time and break open mathematically, geometrically, as it were, much like the waiting bud bursts into the geometric blossom.

Of course, the loosely-emotional ''lover'' of music resents the assertion that his music is mathematics. This means simply that he does not know enough music. Both the physical and emotive bases of music rests in mathematics. The structure of a compound tone is a mathematical phenomenon. Number is finite. And in this instance its content—sound— is also finite. In fact mathematics itself, is but a feeling. Number does not exist in the geographical world outside our own skins. Number is merely a neural feeling of ''nextness.'' On this account music is limited. The history of music becomes a history of exhaustion. Each element of its structure, drawn by inexorable necessity into its vortex is ab-

**208**

sorbed and sucked dry, after which, like a bone thrown to the dog, it is handed over to the theorist.

The development of Teutonic music parallels the structure of a compound tone. The years can be measured in the overtones. The difference is merely a matter of direction. Partial tones are piled up in sequential order, perpendicular, upon the fundamental, while the history of the art itself is worked out in time horizontally, its destiny already decreed by the mathematical formulae of its physical structure. And man swells with pride, thinking that *he* has willed its direction.

But does not man at the same time taste the poison in each potion? Step by step has man not devoured his art in the pleasure of creating it? Because it is called an "Art" are we not beguiled into a false optimism? Merely to change a word is to be enlightened. Instead of "art" let music be called a "Science."

What?

You object?

But music treats neurally with a physical structure as dense and opaque as any "matter" crushed in the scien-

**209**

tist's laboratory. But, one objects, music is feeling. I can only answer "yes." Adding that physics also is feeling. If one does not believe this, one does not know enough physics.

In the beginning is the fundamental tone — the first, partial which becomes the basis for all melodic progression. The second partial—our octave was pillaged in the magadizing of the ancients. In time the third partial—the fifth tone of our diatonic scale and its inversion, the fourth, with all its Byzantine glassiness were absorbed in organum. Eventually the third tone of our scale, the fifth partial—a wholly Teutonic interval and its inversion, the sixth, forbidden in the cold chant of the church were exhausted in soft sentimentalism. After which in chronological order, comes the seventh partial— our minor seventh, moist and slimy. Then later, the major seventh, harsh and biting, the fifteenth partial.

Has this strange phenomenon ever before been noticed —that the minor seventh which structurally precedes the major was also the first to be developed? Proving that mathematics determines destiny.

# 210

In between the development of the two sevenths lies the ninth, not only in time but in structure. The ninth, so thoroughly consumed by the Frenchman is now but the chief reliance of the stupid jazzists.

Finally come the atonalists, those intellectuals who play around in the realms of the higher partials where key relations are acknowledged but no longer felt. And then, just as the whole structure seems about to disintegrate—a tremendous superstructure of distant stellar partials, tones, as distant from the fundamental as the stars are from this earth—comes Arnold Schoenberg. With one stroke he removes the ground tone and creates a new structure such as has never been heard before.

Destiny?

Mathematical destiny.

Before Schoenberg there were two paths into the future. One lay in the direction of smaller and more intervals worked out in the extreme upper partials. Undoubtedly music at some other time had taken this path. Primitive music with its more minute scale subdivisions must therefore, be a remnant of a great but vanished music architecture.

Our music, however, was destined to move in another direction. After Schoenberg there is no choice, so magnificently has the new Form been set forth. There can be no going back. Organic growth is irreversable.

From now on music will no longer be what it was, but has become what it will be. This change can be likened to the change from the Euclidian geometry to the higher mathematics of a Minkowski—an Einstein. Teutonic music was built upon a Euclidian geometric key relation of note to note. The cycle of fifths determines its limits. The new music of Schoenberg is built on a structural principle just as true, just as logical and just as musical. It is built on the relation of number to number—whose total content is sound. By the removal of the tonic Schoenberg freed the upper partials so they can move in any direction determined by the structural feeling of the composer unhampered by key relations. In this rebirth the creator of the times to come will find new paths, new

**212**

destinies, new neural beauty. Music is not so much in-vention *as exploration*.

Schoenberg devoured the past. Satiety could only be avoided by this dangerous but fruitful plunge into the future—the *Twelve-sound structure*. One cannot even use the term Twelve-tone scale because that term still tacitly acknowledges the old system.

It is a metamorphosis.

[1936]

**213**

# NICHOLAS SLONIMSKY

### 13 SEPTEMBER 1874

Arnold Schoenberg is born in Vienna.

### SEPTEMBER 1899

Arnold Schoenberg composes his string sextet, *Verk-laerte Nacht,* in D-minor, op. 4, inspired by the poem of Richard Dehmel from his cycle, "Weib und Welt."

### MARCH 1901

Arnold Schoenberg puts in an order, with the Viennese printers Messrs. Waldheim & Eberle, for special size music paper, sufficiently large to include the choral and orchestral parts of Part III of his *Gurre-Lieder.*

"There is a young man of Vienna who leaves us all behind: he needs sixty-five staves for his score, for which he has his music paper specially printed, and I told him that I myself could not make head or tail of them" (Richard Strauss quoted by Kurt Schindler in his address at the private performance in New York of Schoenberg's D-minor Quartet, 28 December 1913).

## 215

## March 1904

The *Vereinigung Schaffender Tonkuenstler* is formed in Vienna, with Arnold Schoenberg as president, Alexander Zemlinsky, Oskar Posa, Robert Gounod, Erich Wolff, and Joseph V. Woess, as members, with the purpose of promoting free creative art, independent of commercial considerations or newspaper criticisms.

## 26 January 1905

Arnold Schoenberg conducts in Vienna the first performance of his symphonic poem, *Pelleas and Melisande,* to Maeterlinck's play, at a concert organized by the *Vereinigung Schaffender Tonkuenstler.*

"The three leaders of the *Verein der Schaffenden Tonkuenstler,* Arnold Schoenberg, Alexander Zemlinsky, and Oskar Posa devoted an entire evening to their cause. The most talented of them—Schoenberg—was the most unpalatable. Fully fifty minutes takes his continuous symphonic poem, *Pelleas and Melisande.* For the whole fifty minutes one deals with a man either devoid of all sense or one who takes his listeners for fools ... Schoenberg's *opus* is not merely filled with wrong notes, as Strauss' *Don Quixote* is, but is itself a fifty-minute long

**216**

wrong note. This is to be taken literally. What else may hide behind the cacophony is impossible to ascertain." (Ludwig Karpath in *Die Signale*, 1 March 1905).

"A trombone glissando was used for the first time by Schoenberg in his symphonic poem, *Pelleas and Melisande*, full score, p. 51. Here the note E and its octave are fixed as basis of the sixth position by the lips, and the tube is pushed through all the positions in such a way that the intervals of half and quarter tones can be clearly heard." (Egon Wellesz in Hull's *Dictionary of Modern Music and Musicians*, London, 1924).

## 15 FEBRUARY 1907

*D-minor String Quartet*, op. 7, by Arnold Schoenberg, entirely within a tonal frame, as the designation of the key clearly indicates, is performed for the first time in Vienna.

## 9 MARCH 1907

Arnold Schoenberg finishes in Vienna the composition of his choral work, *Friede auf Erden*, op. 13, and begins his work on the *F-sharp Minor String Quartet*, designated op. 10, his last work, chronologically and by opus number, to bear a key signature indicative of tonality.

## 17 DECEMBER 1907

Arnold Schoenberg begins the composition of a suite of songs to Stefan Georg's expressionist poems *Das Buch der Haengenden Gaerten.*

## 22 FEBRUARY 1909

Arnold Schoenberg composes the second piece of the three *Klavierstuecke,* op. 11, which marks the final departure from tonality and the beginning of atonality (not yet the twelve-tone system) with the key-note still remaining in the form of a basso ostinato.

"I am striving toward a goal that seems to be certain, and I already feel the opposition that I shall have to overcome.... It is not lack of invention nor of technical skill, nor the knowledge of the other requirements of contemporary aesthetics that has urged me to this.... I am following an inner compulsion that is stronger than education, stronger than my artistic training." (Arnold Schoenberg in a program note).

## 19 MARCH 1909

Arnold Schoenberg composes No. 1 of the three *Klavierstuecke,* op. 11 in an idiom farther away from tonality, than No. 2 of the same opus number, written twenty-five days before.

## 27 AUGUST 1909

Arnold Schoenberg begins the composition of his mono-drama, *Erwartung,* in which he subtilizes the means of expression to the greatest degree, to correspond with the philosophical idea of simultaneity of the course of life, as seen at the moment of death.

## 12 SEPTEMBER 1909

On the eve of his thirty-fifth birthday, Arnold Schoenberg completes the composition of his monodrama, *Erwartung.*

## SEPTEMBER 1910

Arnold Schoenberg's paintings are put on exhibition at a special showing in a Viennese gallery.

## JULY 1911

Two months before his thirty-seventh birthday, Arnold Schoenberg completes in Vienna his *Harmonielehre* dedicated to the memory of Gustav Mahler.

## 219

"No art has been so hindered in its development by teachers as music, since nobody watches more closely over his property than the man who knows that, strictly speaking, it does not belong to him." (From *Harmonielehre*).

## 7 NOVEMBER 1911

After ten and a half years of intermittent work, Arnold Schoenberg completes, in Zehlendorf, near Berlin, the composition of *Gurre-Lieder* to the poems by the Danish poet, Jens Peter Jacobsen, for five solo voices, three four-part male choirs and a mixed choir of eight parts, a narrator and large orchestra, in three parts:

Part 1, in E-flat major, in sextuple and dodecuple time, vaguely Brucknerian and Straussian in character, also showing selective affinity with Mahler. Part II. Slow and short, in B-flat minor. Part III. *The Wild Hunt,* the longest, and the most chromatic, ending in a joyous diatonic hymn to the rising sun with a twenty-eight-bar long coda in an unergotized C-major.

"The whole composition was finished, I should say, in April or May, 1901. Only the final chorus was still in rough sketches.... Indications of the orchestration were,

**220**

in the original composition, not very numerous. ... In finishing the score, I rewrote only a few passages. Everything else, even a good deal that I would willingly have had otherwise, remained as it was at first." (From Schoenberg's letter to Alban Berg, quoted in Alban Berg's *Guide to Gurre-Lieder*).

### 30 March 1912

Arnold Schoenberg writes the first song of the "Three Times Seven" poems, opus number (significantly!) 21, under the general title *Pierrot Lunaire,* to the symbolist texts by Albert Giraud, translated into German by Hartleben, and scored for a small ensemble of instruments: Flute (also Piccolo), Clarinet (also Bass-Clarinet), Violin, interchangeable with Viola, 'Cello, Piano and a singing-speaking voice (contralto), the first song being thirty-nine unequal bars in length.

### 3 September 1912

Sir Henry Wood conducts at Queen's Hall in London the first performance anywhere of Arnold Schoenberg's *Five Orchestral Pieces,* op. 16.

(1) *Vorgefuehl,* rapid movement melodically based

on fourths, fifths, and tritones in canonical construction; (2) *Vergangenes,* in measured slow time, highly individualized instrumentation with solo passages suggesting, Strauss-like, faces seen and events lived; (3) *Der Wechselnde Akkord,* thematically stationary chord in quartal harmony enveloped in constantly changing instrumental colors; (4) *Peripatetik,* in rapid tempo, in a more astringent, secundal harmony; (5) *Das Obligato Recitativ,* in which a special sign to indicate the principal theme is introduced for the first time.

"This music seeks to express all that dwells in us subconsciously like a dream; which is a great fluctuant power, and is built upon none of the lines that are familiar to us; which has a rhythm, as the blood has its pulsating rhythm, as all life in us has its rhythm; which has a tonality, but only as the sea or the storm has its tonality; which has harmonies, though we cannot grasp or analyze them nor can we trace its themes. All its technical craft is submerged, made one and indivisible with the content of the work." (From the program book).

"We are promised at least one sensation at the Promenade Concerts next week, Arnold Schoenberg's *Five Orchestral Pieces.* To describe Schoenberg as a

**222**

modernist is, apparently, the merest platitude. Not only has he out-Straussed Strauss in his application (or repudiation) of the laws of harmony, but he claims, so we are told, serious consideration as a Futurist painter. The other day he was appointed to a professorship at the Vienna Academy of Music, and friends and foes alike— and he has many of each—are now wondering what sort of composition he is going to teach the students in that institution. His appointment came as a thunderclap to most people acquainted with his extreme methods.'' (London *Daily Mail,* 31 August 1912).

''The program of last Tuesday's Promenade Concert included *Five Orchestral Pieces,* op. 16, by Arnold Schoenberg, who evidently revels in the bizarre. According to Dr. Anton von Webern, his music 'contains the experience of his emotional life,' and that experience must have been of a strange, not to say unpleasant character. . . . Is it really honest music or merely a pose? We are inclined to think the latter. If music at all, it is music of the future, and we hope, of a distant one. There is plenty of interesting and noble music to enjoy. Why, then, should the ears of the Promenade audience be tortured with scrappy sounds and perpetual discord?'' (London *Daily Mail,* 7 September 1912).

''It was like a poem in Tibetan; not one single soul

could possibly have understood it at a first hearing. We can, after all, only progress from the known to the unknown; and as the programme writer, who had every reason to know, said, there was not a single consonance from beginning to end. Under such circumstances the listener was like a dweller in Flatland straining his mind to understand the ways of that mysterious occupant of three dimensions, man.... At the conclusion half the audience hissed. That seems a too decisive judgment, for after all they may turn out to be wrong; the other half applauded more vehemently than the case warranted, for it could hardly have been from understanding.'' (London *Times,* 4 September 1912).

''It is impossible to give an idea of the music. The endless discords, the constant succession of unnatural sounds from the extreme notes of every instrument, and the complete absence of any kind of idea, which, at one hearing at least, one can get hold of, baffle description. Herr Schoenberg, in short, is to Strauss at his wildest what Strauss is to Mozart, and he is never for a bare space normal. He does not even end his pieces with recognizable chords. He is a Futurist painter, and he scores as he paints.'' (*The Manchester Guardian,* 5 September 1912).

''Imagine the scene of the bleating of sheep in 'Don Quixote,' the sacrificial procession in 'Electra,' and the

scene of the opponents in 'Heldenleben' all played together and you will have a faint idea of Schoenberg's
idea of orchestral color and harmony. As to theme or
subject, it must be supposed that he would consider it an
insult to be told that he has any traffic with such things.
... The pieces have no programme or poetic basis. We
must be content with the composer's own assertion that
he has depicted his own experiences, for which he has our
heartfelt sympathy." (*The Daily News,* London, 4 September 1912).

"Schoenberg's music is a return to an elemental condition. It is a collection of sounds without relation to one
another. It is the reproduction of the sounds of nature
in their crudest form. Modern intellect has advanced beyond mere elementary noise: Schoenberg has not. If the
mind of man is superior to that of beast then it should be
able to improve and not rest content with imitation. The
course adopted by Schoenberg is retrograde." (*The
Morning Post,* 4 September 1912).

"It is not often that an English audience hisses the
music it does not like; but a good third of the people at
Queen's Hall the other day permitted themselves that
luxury after the performance of the five orchestral pieces
of Schoenberg. Another third of the audience was not
hissing because it was laughing, and the remaining third
seemed too puzzled either to laugh or to hiss. ... Never-

theless, I take leave to suggest that Schoenberg is not the mere fool or madman that he is generally supposed to be. ... May it not be that the new composer sees a logic in certain tonal relations that to the rest of us seem chaos at present, but the coherence of which may be clear enough to us all some day?" (Ernest Newman in the London *Nation,* September, 1912).

## 9 SEPTEMBER 1912

After 164 days of intermittent work, Arnold Schoenberg completes, four days before his thirty-eighth birthday, the cycle of "Three Times Seven" songs, *Pierrot Lunaire,* containing $(39+41+31+18+44+24+27 = 224) + (26+20+20+29+13+36+22 = 166) + (31+27+32+19+53+30+30 = 222) = 612$ unequal bars in quarter-note meters (except in *Parodie* and *Heimfahrt,* which are in eighth-note meters).

## 16 OCTOBER 1912

After forty rehearsals Arnold Schoenberg's *Pierrot Lunaire,* "set to tones" *(vertont)* for speaking voice and chamber orchestra is performed for the first time anywhere, in the Choralionsaal in Berlin, with Albertine

Zehme, to whom the work is dedicated, as singing narrator.

## "A 'METAMUSICAL' EVENING. ARNOLD SCHOENBERG'S 'LIEDER DES PIERROT LUNAIRE.'

Herman Helmholz speaks somewhere about so-called 'metamathematical spaces,' that is, spaces wherein the known axioms of Euclid's geometry are not valid. I think of these remarkable spaces when I tread on the tone-space of latest Schoenberg: I feel translated into 'metamusical spaces.' To breathe in this new atmosphere, one must leave behind all that is considered axiomatic in things musical. One must first learn the new alphabet to approach this new frightful Schoenberg, to get the bearings of this 'Prose of Music,' as Herr von Webern calls it. . . . Outwardly the evening in the Choralionsaal was very, very interesting. And there was virtually no hissing. Perhaps, the audience was an invited one." (Pisling in *Die Signale*, 2 November 1912).

"Schoenberg's music to Albert Giraud's fantastical poems entitled *Pierrot Lunaire* is the last word in cacophony and musical anarchy. Some day it may be pointed out as of historical interest, because it represents the turning point, for the outraged muse surely can endure no more of this. Such noise must drive even the moonstruck Pierrot back to the realm of real music. Albertina Zehme, a well-known Berlin actress, dressed in a Pierrot costume, recited the 'Three Times Seven' poems, while a musical, or, rather, unmusical ensemble, consisting of a piano, violin, viola, 'cello, piccolo, and clarinet, stationed behind a black screen and invisible to the audience, discoursed the most ear-splitting combinations of tones that ever desecrated the walls of a Berlin music hall.'' (Berlin correspondence of the *Musical Courier,* November, 1912).

"If this is music of the future, then I pray my Creator not to let me live to hear it again.'' (Otto Taubman in the *Boersen Courier, Berlin,* November, 1912).

"In Berlin I had an occasion to hear Schoenberg's music for the first time, when he invited me to attend a performance of his *Pierrot Lunaire.* I was not at all enthusiastic over the estheticism of this work which seemed to me a reversion to the superannuated cult of Beardsley. But, as an instrumental achievement, the score of *Pierrot Lunaire* is unquestionably a success.'' (Stravinsky, *Chroniques de ma Vie,* Paris, 1935).

### 21 DECEMBER 1912

Arnold Schoenberg conducts the first Russian performance of his symphonic poem *Pelleas and Melisande,* at a Siloti concert in St. Petersburg.

### 23 FEBRUARY 1913

Fifteen and a half months after the completion of the score of Arnold Schoenberg's *Gurre-Lieder,* Franz Schreker conducts in Vienna the first performance of the work.

"There was an orchestra of one hundred and forty pieces, including chimes, gongs, weird sounding trumpets and even a huge iron chain. Four choruses were called into action — three of men's voices and one of mixed voices—making in all a total of nearly four hundred persons on the stage." *(Musical Courier,* Vienna Despatch, March, 1913).

### 24 FEBRUARY 1913

At the performance of Arnold Schoenberg's *Pierrot Lunaire* in Prague, a noisy demonstration of protest is staged by a section of the audience.

### 31 MARCH 1913

The Academic Society for Literature and Music in

**229**

Vienna presents a concert of first performances of music by Arnold Schoenberg's pupil, Anton von Webern (*Six Orchestral Pieces*); Schoenberg's teacher and brother-in-law, Alexander Zemlinsky *(Four Orchestral Songs to Maeterlinck's Poems)*; Schoenberg himself, (*Kammersymphonie,* op. 9, for fifteen solo instruments, in one continuous movement, well within the indicated tonality, E-major, and thematically based on rows of perfect fourths), and Alban Berg *(Two Orchestral Songs to Texts of Picture Postcards).*

''The Grosser Musikvereinsall audience has an air of expectancy. Vienna prides itself on being 'advanced,' and this is no joke either. There are more things possible with the modern orchestra, so we find out, than Strauss ever dreamed of. These strange whimpers and sighs, the growls of the basses underneath the peculiar wheezes which the clarinetist can produce if he presses his lower lip in a certain way—can they be the birth pangs of a new art, these zoological expressions that would make the real menagerie seek cover with drooping tails and ears in their general disgust at nature's provision to them of such inadequate vocal talents? As for the key — gracious! people wrote in 'keys' far back in

1910. We thought we knew all the discords which human ingenuity could devise, but here even the wisest can learn something. It is without doubt 'original' music. It is, to be specific, the music of some of Schoenberg's pupils being performed at the concert of March 31 given under the auspices of the *Akademischer Verband fuer Literatur und Musik* with the master himself conducting. They may be called 'Ultralists,' though by any other name they could by no means lose any of their fragrance.... If this concert was intended to be a 'memorable occasion,' it surely succeeded, for it occasioned the greatest uproar which has occured in a Vienna concert hall in the memory of the oldest critics writing. Laughter, hisses, and applause continued throughout a great part of the actual performance of the disputed pieces. After the Berg songs the dispute became almost a riot. The police were sought and the only officer who could be found actually threw out of the gallery one noisemaker who persisted in blowing on a key for a whistle. But this policeman could not prevent one of the composers from appearing in a box and yelling to the crowd, 'Heraus mit der Baggage!' (Out with the trash!) Whereat the uproar increased. Members of the orchestra descended from the stage and entered into spirited controversy with the audience. And finally the president of the *Akademischer Verband* came and boxed the ears of a man who had insulted him while he was making an announcement.'' (Vienna despatch in the *Musical Courier,* 23 April 1913).

**231**

### 6 OCTOBER 1913

Arnold Schoenberg composes in Berlin the first of the *Four Songs* for voice and orchestra, op. 22, to a poem by Stefan Georg, *Seraphita,* eighty-five unequal bars in length.

### 18 NOVEMBER 1913

Two months and five days after his thirty-ninth birthday, Arnold Schoenberg completes the score of *Die Glueckliche Hand,* expressionist monodrama, to his own text, making use of color dynamics. (Thus *crescendo* in the orchestra is accompanied by a *crescendo* of colors: red, brown, green, dark blue, purple).

### 19 NOVEMBER 1913

The Violoncello Concerto by Johann Cristoph Monn, freely arranged by Arnold Schoenberg with cembalo and small orchestra accompaniment, is performed for the first time at a concert in Vienna on the occasion of the twentieth anniversary of the series *Denkmaeler Der Tonkunst in Oesterreich,* with Pablo Casals playing the 'cello solo part.

Arnold Schoenberg conducts his *Five Orchestral Pieces* in his first appearance in London.

"LONDON BAFFLED BY SCHOENBERG'S ORCHESTRAL PIECES—Composer Himself Conducts His Work and He at Least is Pleased—Reminiscent of a Nightmare." *(Musical America,* February 1914).

"CRITICS IN LONDON RAP FUTURIST MUSIC—Herr Schoenberg's Composition Called 'Vague, Scrappy, and Incoherent.' 'Incomprehensible Noise.' Viennese Composer Writes in Hierogliphics, says one newspaper." *(New York Sun,* February, 1914).

"To the Editor of 'The Daily Telegraph': Sir: Any one acquainted with music history would find little cause for surprise at the incoherent criticism following on the performance of the Schoenberg Compositions at Queen's Hall. The vulgarity of the writer who stated that 'long hair used to be indispensable has now been superseded by the bald head' (an obvious and disgraceful attack on the personality of Herr Schoenberg) and the even more stupid remark of the other person who wrote that 'they (the Schoenberg pieces) were so ridiculous in their chaotic formlessness that the orchestra sometimes laughed down their instruments instead of blowing down

**233**

them' may be dismissed as examples of ignorance and lack of decency. It is, however, surprising to find ... this bewilderment on the part of our more sincere critics. May I venture to suggest that it is a lack of constructive vision in regard to musical psychology?'' (From a letter by Leigh Henry to the editor of the *Daily Telegram,* 17 February 1914).

### 28 AUGUST 1914

Arnold Schoenberg composes in Berlin, his song *Vorgefuehl,* one of the *Four Songs* for voice and orchestra, op. 22, to a poem by Rainer Maria Rilke, twenty-seven unequal bars in length, making use of *vocal harmonics* (head-tones).

### 3 DECEMBER 1914

Arnold Schoenberg composes, in Berlin, the third in order of the *Four Songs* for voice and orchestra, op. 22, to a poem by Ranier Maria Rilke, thirty-nine unequal bars in length.

### 1 JANUARY 1915

Arnold Schoenberg composes the last (second in the order) of the *Four Songs,* for voice and orchestra, op. 22, twenty-five unequal bars in length, to a poem of Rainer Maria Rilke.

## NOVEMBER 1918

Arnold Schoenberg founds in Vienna a Society for Private Musical Performances (*Verein fuer Musikalische Privatauffuehrungen in Wien*) for the purpose of giving artists and music-lovers a real and exact knowledge of modern music, free from the corrupting influence of publicity, with newspaper critics barred from attendance, the applause or hissing forbidden, and the members pledged to give no public report of the proceedings.

Any person of honorable and unblemished character willing to accept the regulations of the Society may become a member.

The members of the Society are obligated:

*a)* to further the aims of the Society and to avoid acts prejudicial to them.

*b)* to pay membership dues for the current year, even in case of premature cessation of membership.

*c)* not to injure the cause served by the Society.

**235**

The direction of the Society consists of:

*a)* the President, Arnold Schoenberg, the duration of whose tenure is not limited.

*b)* a Committee of from ten to twenty members (chairman, secretary, etc.), chosen by the General Assembly in agreement with the President.

The President has a completely free hand in the direction of the Society. He decides upon the kind and amount of the expenditures necessary to the work of the Society. He has also the right to remit wholly or in part the dues of worthy and needy members.

All decisions of the General Assembly, including elections, changes in statutes, dissolution of the Society, etc., require for their validity, the consent of the President.

(From the Statutes of the Society).

### 16 FEBRUARY 1919

Arnold Schoenberg issues a declaration of aims of the *Verein Fuer Musikalische Privatauffuerungen* in Vienna.

### 7 DECEMBER 1922

Bach's *Two Choral Preludes,* orchestrated by Arnold

Schoenberg, are performed for the first time by the New York Philharmonic Orchestra, under the direction of Josef Stransky.

## 6 JUNE 1924

Arnold Schoenberg's melodrama *Erwartung,* op. 17, expressionist cantata with a single acting part is performed for the first time at the conclusion of the Prague Festival of Contemporary Music.

## 20 JULY 1924

The *Gesellschaft der Musikfreunde zu Donaueschingen* presents, in the course of the fourth festival of chamber music, the first public performance of Arnold Schoenberg's opus 24, the epoch-making *Serenade,* for Violin, 'Cello, Clarinet, Bass Clarinet, Mandolin, Guitar and deep voice, the first work in which the twelve-tone system is firmly established, the themes being built on twelve non-repeated notes while the form remains that of the classical Suite:

(1) *March,* (2) *Minuet,* (3) *Variations,* (4) *Sonnet* of Petrarca (in which the row of twelve tones appears in the

voice as a melody, in the accompaniment, as motives, in harmony as complete chords) (5) *Tanzszene,* (6) *Lied Ohne Worte,* (7) *Finale,* a modified recapitulation of the inaugural March.

### 13 SEPTEMBER 1924

Friends and deciples of Arnold Schoenberg publish a dedicatory volume of 324 pages for his fiftieth birthday, containing articles by Anton von Webern, Alban Berg, and Paul Bekker, and testimonials from Casella, Malipiero; also samples of abusive newspaper articles published without comment; and Universal Edition opens an *Arnold Schoenberg Library* of modern music, accessible to students free of charge. On the same day Schoenberg's *Quintet* for Flute, Oboe, Clarinet, Bassoon, and Horn, written in the strictest twelve-tone code, and in an equally strict sonata form, is performed for the first time anywhere, in Vienna.

### 14 OCTOBER 1924

Arnold Schoenberg's *Die Glueckliche Hand,* op. 18, drama with music, is performed in Vienna, nearly eleven years after the completion of the score.

# 238

### 6 DECEMBER 1925

The Academy Santa Cecilia in Rome confers honorary membership on Arnold Schoenberg.

### 2 JULY 1927

At the second chamber concert of the Frankfort Festival, the logical, austere, and yet emotionally tense *Chamber Concerto* for Piano, Violin, and thirteen Wind-instruments by Alban Berg, based on the anagrammatic arrangement of letters in the name of Arnold Schoenberg (ADESCBEG), is performed for the first time.

### 19 SEPTEMBER 1927

Six days after Arnold Schoenberg's fifty-third birthday, his *Third String Quartet,* op. 30, based on the system of twelve tones in free style, with repetition of notes in transitional or introductory passages, is performed for the first time in public by the Kolisch String Quartet in Vienna.

### 20 SEPTEMBER 1928

A week after his fifty-fourth birthday Arnold Schoen-

**239**

berg completes at Roquebourne, the score of his *Variations for Orchestra,* op. 31, on a theme of twelve different tones (''row''): B-flat, F-flat, G-flat, E-flat, F, A, D, C-sharp, G, G-sharp, B and C, treated in inversion, retrograde motion, and vertical integration.

### 2 DECEMBER 1928

*Variations for Orchestra,* op. 31, by Arnold Schoenberg are performed for the first time in Berlin. Wilhelm Furtwaengler conducting.

''The majority of the audience was silent, but two excited minorities engaged in combat. The give-and-take of remarks for and against the piece grew to greater dimensions and took more unfortunate forms than we have ever experienced at a Schoenberg premiere. And we are accustomed to almost anything. (Max Marschalk in *Die Vossische Zeitung*).

### 3 AUGUST 1929

Arnold Schoenberg completes *Von Heute auf Morgen,* one-act opera to the expressionist text by Max Blonda, making use of Saxophones and a Flexaton in addition to the usual orchestra.

**240**

## 10 November 1929

The orchestration of Bach's Prelude and Fugue for Organ, in E-flat major by Arnold Schoenberg is performed for the first time in Vienna, Anton von Webern conducting.

## 14 February 1930

Arnold Schoenberg completes, in Berlin, the composition of his score for small orchestra, *Begleitungsmusik zu einer Lichtspielszene,* (accompaniment to a Cinema Scene), in one continuous movement, subdivided into three cinematographically effective sections, along a fine scale of dynamics: *Drohende Gefahr, Angst, Katastrophe,* in the strictest twelve-tone technique, with the following tone-row within a two-bar period: E-flat, G-flat, D, E, C-sharp, C, B, A, B-flat, A-flat, G, F.

## 30 May 1933

Arnold Schoenberg is dismissed from the faculty of the Prussian Academy of Arts by order of the German Ministry of Education, as not meeting the requirements of the Aryan paragraph.

**241**

### 23 July 1933

*Begleitungsmusik zu einer Lichtspielszene,* Arnold Schoenberg's first symphonic work which portrays cinematic emotions as indicated in the subtitles, *Drohende Gefahr, Angst* and *Katastrophe,* is performed for the first time in the cinema capital at a "Twilight" Sunday concert by the Hollywood Bowl Orchestra, Nicolas Slonimsky conducting.

### 24 July 1933

At the ceremony in a Paris synagogue, Arnold Schoenberg returns to the Hebrew faith, which he abandoned in 1921.

### 31 October 1933

Arnold Schoenberg arrives in America to teach at the Malkin Conservatory in Boston.

### 11 November 1933

The League of Composers presents in New York a concert of Arnold Schoenberg's chamber music, in celebration of his arrival in America.

**242**

## 13 September 1934

On the occasion of Arnold Schoenberg's sixtieth birthday, a dedicatory volume is published by Universal Edition, with a poem by Schoenberg himself, *Verbundenheit,* an anagrammatic poem by Alban Berg, spelling *Glaube, Hoffnung und Liebe,* and articles by Anton von Webern, Alois Hába, Egon Wellesz, Erwin Stein, Darius Milhaud, Alexander Zemlinsky, Alma Mahler, Hans Erich Apostel, Paul Stefan, Willi Reich, Paul A. Pisk, David Josef Bach and others.

## 26 December 1934

Arnold Schoenberg completes in Hollywood his *Suite* for strings in G-major, the first key signature indicative in a definite tonality he put on paper since 9 March 1907.

"I was incited to write this work by a musician who is a teacher at the New York University and conducts a pupil's orchestra. He told me much that was most gratifying about these American orchestras of which there are many hundreds. This piece, therefore, will provide instructive examples of progressions which are possible within tonality to any genuine musician who knows his craft; an actual preparation, not only from a harmonic,

**243**

but also from a melodic, contrapuntal and technical stand-point." (From Arnold Schoenberg's letter to Erwin Stein, November, 1934).

### 18 MAY 1935

Arnold Schoenberg's *Suite* for String Orchestra, in five movements of the classical suite, is performed for the first time by the Los Angeles Philharmonic Orchestra, Otto Klemperer conducting.

### 26 JULY 1936

Arnold Schoenberg completes in Hollywood the composition of his fourth *String Quartet,* op. 37, in four movements, within the frame of the strict twelve-tone system, in lyrical melodic treatment.

### 23 SEPTEMBER 1936

Ten days after his sixty-second birthday, Arnold Schoenberg completes in Hollywood the composition of his *Violin Concerto,* op. 36.

### 9 JANUARY 1937

Arnold Schoenberg's *String Quartet,* op. 37, is performed by the Kolisch Quartet during the course of a Schoenberg-Beethoven cycle at the University of California of Los Angeles, under the auspices of the Elizabeth Sprague Coolidge Foundation.

## 17 FEBRUARY 1937

Arnold Schoenberg's symphonic poem *"Pelleas and Melisande"* is performed by the Federal Music Project Symphony Orchestra in Los Angeles, with the composer conducting.

## MAY 1937

Merle Armitage of Los Angeles publishes for G. Schirmer, Inc., of New York, a dedicatory volume to Arnold Schoenberg, containing articles by American and European musicians and a chronology of Schoenberg's career.

[1937]

**245**

# AFFIRMATIONS

It is not at all difficult for the artist to say something about his creations if he only observes falsely. Then everything presents itself simply, according to taste, either classically simple or romantically complicated; a clear path will be traversed; goals are reached or sighted; manner is style, style, personality, personality — Redeemer or Lucifer—all according to taste; in any case, everything is so much a matter of course that the sleekest biographer could accomplish it no more smoothly. It is possible that there are artists who live out their patterned biographies with such care, manifest the same sense of duty toward broken laws as do others toward respected, who form a shackle from every freedom, who none the less are unable, in the consciousness of the shackles on their innermost laws, to feel themselves free. When creators of this kind are artists, one may envy them the blindness which permits them to see such smoothness.

●

**247**

When after a period of rest, full of desire for work, I think of coming projects, my future course always lies so clearly ahead of me that nowadays, at least, I can be certain that it will be different from that of my conception. That I turn, perhaps revolve, revolve whirlingly, is still conjecturable; only my blindness may be blamed for not perceiving where I stand, where I stood. But one thing soon becomes clear: that the new appears just as strange and incomprehensible as formerly the old; that as long as this condition lasts, the old becomes more comprehensible, until finally the new in turn grows apparently in my confidence and I cease to understand how I formerly could have written otherwise than thus.

Yes, when one observes well, these things gradually become obscure. One begins to realize that one is not destined only not to guess the future (only to delineate it) but also, to forget the past, already set forth. One wins a feeling of the most faithful carrying out of one's duty when, although wishing otherwise, one does not do what appeared holy in the past and begins quietly to rejoice over one's blindness with seeing eyes.

Very seldom—though, and very secretly for a solitary moment, the finished work, and that still to be finished, has been suddenly sighted and one was satisfied.

●

A problematic relationship between the science of mathematics as expressed by Einstein and the science of music as developed by myself?

There may be a relationship in the two fields of endeavor, but I have no idea what it is. I write music as music without any reference other than to express my feelings in tone. I do not shape my scores with a definite idea to express anything but music. All symbolic ideas are read into it by musicologists, for I have no intention when I write of solving tonal problems, creating emotional response or building unusual patterns. All I want to do is to express my thoughts and get the most possible content in the least possible space.

●

If a composer doesn't write from the heart, he simply can't produce good music... I have never had a theory in my life. I get a musical idea for a composition, I try to develop it into a certain logical and beautiful conception, and I try to clothe it in a type of music which exudes from me naturally and inevitably. I don't consciously create a tonal or polytonal or polyplanal music. I write what I feel in my heart—and what finally comes on paper is what first coursed through every fibre of my body. It is for this reason I cannot tell anyone what the style of my next composition will be. For its style will be whatever I feel when I develop and elaborate my ideas.

I offer incontestable proof of the fact that in following the twelve-tone scale, a composer is neither less nor more bound, hindered nor made independent. He may be as cold-hearted and unmoved as an engineer or, as laymen imagine, may conceive in sweet dreams . . . in inspiration.

What can be constructed with these twelve tones depends on one's inventive faculty. The basic tones will not invent for you. Expression is limited only by the composer's creativeness and his personality. . . He may be original or moving, with old or modern methods. Finally, success depends only on whether we are touched, excited, made happy, enthusiastic . . . or not.

## 250

The tempest raised about my music does not rest upon my ideas, but exists because of the dissonances. Dissonances are but consonances which appear later among the overtones.

●

No one can say this way is absolutely and unqualifiedly right. We do not know whether Schiller or Goethe, Wagner or Mozart is the greater. Final values are yet to be determined, though I think we strive always towards the same—universality of soul, perhaps!

●

I am but the loud-speaker of an idea. The idea is an electric current—in the air. It may come from Jupiter—from the cosmos—that is not proven.

●

I think it would have been better for me, personally, to have written another music than these later works. I was content as I wrote in the period of the Kammer Symphony. But I hardly had written so, until I began to compose in a new style without knowing it. In the time of the Kammer Symphony, I understood better what I

**251**

had written and I had more personal pleasure with that, than with the music which followed.

Then to compose was a great pleasure. In a later time it was a duty against myself. It was not a question of pleasure. I have a mission—a task ... I am but the loud-speaker of an idea!

I was utterly ashamed a few years ago when I discovered that I had no idea of what was going on in the poems underlying several familiar Schubert songs. But when I had read the poems, I found that my understanding of the songs had gained nothing thereby and that I was in no way compelled to alter my conception of their interpretation. On the contrary, it became evident to me, that the content, the real content, had been better comprehended than if I had adhered merely to the superficial content of the literal word procedure.

It became clear to me that the same relationship existed between a work of art and any perfect organism. It is so homogeneous in its synthesis that its every particle discloses its truest, inmost being. If one cuts into any part of the human body, the same substance (blood) appears. When one hears one verse of a poem, one measure of a piece of music, one is in a position to comprehend the whole. Thus I had understood perfectly Schubert's songs along with their poems, from the music alone, and Stefan Georg's poems, merely from their sound, with a perfection that could hardly have been approached, much less exceeded, through analysis and synthesis.

To be sure, such impressions subsequently turn to the intellect and demand of it that it arrange them for convenient use; that it dissect, sort, measure and test; that it at any time separate into expressible particles what one possesses as a whole but cannot use. To be sure, artistic creation often makes this detour before it arrives at actual conception. But there are indications that even the other arts, whose substance is apparently more tangible, are surmounting the belief in the omnipotence of the intellect and consciousness. And when Karl Kraus calls speech the mother of thought, Wassily Kandinsky and Oskar Kokoschka paint pictures in which the material provides little more than an opportunity to improvise in colors and forms, and express themselves as heretofore

**253**

only musicians have, these are symptoms of a gradually spreading recognition of the intrinsic virtue of art.

●

(In 1909 Schoenberg gave the public the "Buch der hängenden Gärten," Op. 15, for voice and piano accompaniment, to which he added an apologia whose substance is as follows):

The melodies of Stefan Georg have allowed me to reach for the first time an ideal of form and expression which I long desired. Until today I had neither the strength of mind nor the mastery of my medium to achieve it. But I am the slave of an internal power stronger than my education; it compels me to obey a conception which, inborn, has greater power over me than even any elemental artistic formation.

●

In his "Harmonielehre" (Treatise on Harmony), Schoenberg has written in the preface:

"The book I have learned from my pupils... The mistakes they made when I gave them insufficient or inadequate directions taught me how to teach them rightly.

**254**

Problems correctly solved have proved the rightness of my endeavors, without inducing the erroneous belief on my part that I had really solved the problems thereby, and it seems to me that neither my pupils nor myself have suffered. Had I told them no more than I knew myself, then they too would have known only that and nothing more. As it is, they may even know less. But they do know the main thing, and that is to seek!''

•

There are relatively few persons who are able to understand music, merely from the purely musical point of view. The assumption that a musical piece must awaken images of some description or other and that if it does not, it has not been understood or is worthless, is as generally held as only the false and banal can be. On no other art is a similar demand made; one is satisfied with the effects of their substance, whereby, to be sure, the material of the represented object of itself meets the limited comprehensive. grasp of the middle-class mentality halfway. Since music, as such, lacks a directly rec-

**255**

ognizable material, some seek pure formal beauty in its effects; others, poetic proceedings.

There is no such distinction as old and modern music, but only good music and bad. All music, in so far as it is the product of a truly creative mind, is *new*. Bach is just as *new* today as he ever was—a continual revelation. Truly good things are new. I warn you of the dangers lurking in the die-hard reaction against romanticism. The old romanticism is dead, long live the new! The composer of today without some trace of romanticism in his heart must be lacking in something fundamentally human. On the other hand, music essentially consists of ideas. Beethoven called himself a "brain-proprietor." It is no use to rail at new music because it contains too many ideas. Music without ideas is un-thinkable, and people who are not willing to use their brains to understand music which cannot be fully grasped at the first hearing, are simply lazy-minded. Every true work of art, to be understood has to be thought about; otherwise it has no inherent life. Style in music arises spontaneously out of the exigencies of form; it cannot be decreed. The solu-

**256**

tion of a problem in style is an end in itself. Therefore art remains for art's sake.

Beauty ... is intangible; for it is only present when one whose intuitive power is strong enough to produce it, creates something by virtue of this intuitive power, and he creates something new every time he exercises that power. Beauty is the result of intuition; when the one ceases to be, the other ceases also. The other form of beauty that one can have, which consists of fixed rules and fixed forms, is merely the yearning of one who is unproductive. For the artist this is of secondary importance, as indeed is every accomplishment, since the artist is content with aspiration, whereas the mediocre must have beauty. And yet the artist attains beauty without willing it, for he is only striving after truthfulness.

●

I will not show you that my music is beautiful. You know it not ... I know it.

●

**257**

If you choose to listen to the wave, you must accept what the wave brings.

●

EDITORS NOTE: The foregoing statements were selected from various printed interviews with Schoenberg, in both Europe and America, and arranged to give continuity.

[1933-1934]

258

# ARNOLD SCHOENBERG

In a newspaper I read that a group of modern composers have decreed that tonality must be restored, as, without it, form cannot exist. That it is necessary to re-establish tonality, I do not believe. However, I think it is possible that it will be done, because the belief in technique and its material accompaniments is so deeply rooted that the "Eaiseure" would certainly sooner attempt to move mountains than risk adventures in more mental regions. That the harmonic alone is form-determining is a widely spread delusion, probably just because I already have refuted it in my "Manual of Harmony" (Harmonielehre). It certainly can be drawn upon as an aid to form; but music that does not consist of joints and parts is to be attained by a very different method. My pupils will be able to confirm the fact that in teaching it was my chief endeavor to make clear to them the difference between the formative potentialities of principal and second subjects, introductions, tran-

**259**

sitions, and codas. And they will remember that I always maintained that most of the composers of today are able to write only introductions—able only to place one thing next to another.

The art of giving a true and varied expression to a muscial thought is very little known. Today the majority strive for "style, technique, and sound"; meaning thereby something purely external and therefore merely striking in character, for the sake of which all the old culture displaced in presenting a thought is neglected. And yet we only need take, for example, an older novel of Dickens and note the complex structure and treatment, the cleverly woven threads, and we become conscious of the knowledge that is really necessary for a work of art. The primitive art of merely presenting thoughts, belongs wholly to the uneducated, who only can relate in orderly succession things just as they happen, those who have no grasp of the whole, who can therefore neither anticipate nor go back, nor connect one sentence with another except by means of the copula "and"... "and then I said ... and then he said ... and then we laughed ... and ...

**260**

and so on.'' The narrative goes on only because the story that is being told goes on, because a continuous action drives the story-teller on. The climax is then naturally only dynamic, as its cause is merely extraneous.

It would, however, be a mistake to think that a more artistic expression is only a matter of using a certain technique. I have worked for more than ten years on this, to settle these differences theoretically, and so far successful am I that the work in question will soon be written. But I can say that it is really in the mental realm—where musical thought must be rich in variety—that an artistic expression is possible. The unthinking do not demand it, do not even allow it, and would only feel doubtful if they did it. But they simply do not think.

In my youth a feeling for form was still very alive which, without theoretical explanation, told one how a principal subject was to be formed. ''This sentence rambles,'' was a criticism one might often hear. Brahms was not the last who possessed this art. Mahler and Strauss also have inherited it. Most of those who follow are not even conscious of what it is all about.

**261**

In my "Manual of Harmony" I also analyze the function of tonality and show what the tasks of a composer are who wishes to make use of this medium. Tonality does not only serve, on the contrary it demands to be served. And that is not so simple as the decreeing committee thinks. I am probably the last of the modern composers who has occupied himself with tonal harmony in the sense of the older masters. That this circumstance is not heeded nor understood is not my fault. Those who examine in my first quartet, or in the Kammersymphony, the relation of the keys to each other, and to the incident harmony, would get from them some conception of the demands that are made, in the modern sense, on the tonal development of a harmonic idea. Perhaps they also would understand why a step must be taken from thence onwards, which the critics in question gladly would reverse.

Why does this clique make decrees? I, if I wanted to write with profit on tonality, should neither decree it nor write about it—but reverse it. Were I compelled to write such a work, I would write it first and then perhaps—

NO! not even then. Listeners must have ears, and ears to detect the difference between music and shibboleths.

When I hear these particular pieces in which are avoided all possible tonal non-relationships, or those at least not developed to the end (or similar passages, many of which might be taken for codas) through an F-sharp or C-major triad—according to the mood—then I always think of those savage black potentates who wear only a cravat and a top-hat.

The form of a composition is achieved because: (1) a body exists, and because (2) the members exercise different functions and are created for these functions. He who from the outside forces, through some function on them all, reminds one of the bad craftmen who, to hide faults of construction, over-upholster, over-daub, over-lacquer, cover with nickel, and so on.

Who can say today how a principal subject must be built up? What must one do that it may hold together? that one does not find oneself suddenly on the wrong track? Who can say how a fluid form is solidified? how an introduction, or a development must be evolved? He who

**263**

can do these things and knows will not be in doubt as to whether or not tonality must be restored to achieve form.

I know that the majority is incapable of accomplishing this with the simplest harmony. And I know that construction, formation, superstructure—in one word, artistic expression—does not depend on any technical trick, but lies rather in musical thought itself. He who really thinks, and thinks deeply, will, with different musical ideas, produce different expressions.

All honor to these composers in their desire for form! but they have to look yet further afield in the resources of the art of music when they aspire to higher forms.

[1936]

**264**

# ARNOLD SCHOENBERG

Modern music has centered interest on two problems: that of tonality, and that of dissonance. It cannot be said that the conflict regarding these questions is new, nor that it is waged with new weapons. On the contrary: just as all the battle-fields of world history are constantly the scene of renewed strife, so, too, is this one; this also is a battlefield in the historic sense.

Of course, it is not necessary for me to cite as proof the well-known precedents from the musical past. It is enough to recall the "Dissonance" Quartet of Mozart and Hans Sach's lines:—

> Ihr schlosset nicht im gleichen Ton,
> Das macht den Meistern Pein;
> Doch nimmt Hans Sachs die Lehr' davon;
> Im Lenz wohl müss' es so sein.
> [Your closing key is not the same,
> This gives the masters pain;
> But Hans Sachs draws a rule from this;
> In Spring it must be so, 'tis plain.]

**265**

In Spring!

We can say that in the development of art, it must always be as it is in Spring! One does what is necessary, though it cause somebody else pain; one does what the situation demands, unconcerned about the approval or disapproval of others.

And the cause of music demands, as the history of art-battles shows, that the secret of the sounding tone be always pursued anew. The development of music is more dependent than any other art upon the development of its technic. A truly new idea—at least as musical history reveals—is hardly imaginable without significant changes in musical technic. The material of music offers inexhaustible possibilities; but every new possibility in turn demands a new kind of treatment, because it presents new problems or at any rate demands a new solution of the old one. Every tonal progression, every progression of even two tones, raises a problem which requires a special solution. Yet the further such tones are brought into relation and contrast with each other and with rhythm, the greater is the number of possible solutions

**266**

to the problem, and the more complex are the demands made on the carrying out of the musical idea.

In no art, properly speaking, can one say "the same thing," the same thing which has been said once before, least of all in music.

An idea in music consists principally in the relation of tones to one another. But ever relationship that has been used too often, no matter how extensively modified, must finally be regarded as exhausted; it ceases to have power to convey a thought worthy of expression. Therefore every composer is obliged to invent, to invent new things, to present new tone relations for discussion and to work out their consequences. It is for this reason that the technic of music must develop so quickly and so persistently. In a methodic progression from the more simple to the more complex, one would hardly be aware of the inevitable changes in technic. But imagination does not ask about method nor does it invent according to a graduated scale. Differences in technic therefore appear far more abrupt than they are in reality. When we realize that today the difference in the technic of the early

**267**

Beethoven from that of the later is apparent only to the connoisseur, we can no longer understand the cry from the gallery at the premiere of Beethoven's *Eighth Symphony:* ''Es fällt ihm schon wieder nichts ein.''

As I have said, the battle today, as always in music, is fought for the cause of dissonance and tonality, around concepts that are not even now clearly enough defined. For the phenomena which they are intended to reveal have been in continuous development since the beginning of music. This compels us always to conceive them in a new way. Therefore we shall try in the main to define them in relation to our time, according to present conditions, without claiming eternal validity.

•

Let us first examine the concept of tonality.

This coincides to a certain extent with that of the key, in so far as it refers not merely to the relation of the tones with one another, but much more to the particular way in which all tones relate to a fundamental tone, especially the fundamental tone of the scale, whereby tonality is always comprehended in the sense of a par-

**268**

ticular scale. Thus, for example, we speak of a C-major tonality, etc.

If however, we wish to investigate what the relation of tones to each other really is, the first question that arises is: what makes it possible that a second tone should follow a first, a beginning tone? How is this logically possible?

The question is more important than it seems at first; nevertheless to my knowledge it has not previously been raised. Although all imaginable and far-reaching problems have been considered, no one has yet asked: How, after all, can two tones be joined one with another?

My answer is that such a juxtaposition of tones, if a connection is to be brought about from which a piece of music may be the result, is only possible because a relation already exists between the tones themselves.

Logically, we can only join things that are related, directly or indirectly. In a piece of music I cannot establish a relation between a tone and, let us say, an eraser; simply because no musical relation exists.

To elucidate the relationship between tones one must

first of all recall that every tone is a compound sound, consisting of a fundamental tone (the strongest sounding one) and a series of overtones. We may now make the statement, and to a great extent test and prove it, that all musical phenomena can be referred to the overtone series, so that all things appear to be the application of the more simple and more complex relationships of this series.

Considered singly these relations are as follows:—

1. The major scale is to be explained as nothing else than the addition of the tones of the three main triads on the I, IV and V degrees. In C-major they are, on the I degree: c-e-g; IV degree: f-a-c; V degree g-b-d. But these tones again are nothing other than the fourth, fifth and sixth overtones of the three main fundamentals of a scale, (dominant, tonic, sub-dominant) which the following table demonstrates:

| 1 | 2 | 3 | 4 | 5 | 6 | 7 | 8 | 9 | 10 | 11 | 12 | 13 |
|---|---|---|---|---|---|---|---|---|----|----|----|----|
| C | C | ⌈G⌉ | c | e | g | b♭ | c | d | e | f♯ | g | a♭ |
| F | F | \|C\| | f | a | c | e♭ | f | g | a | b | c | d♭ |
| G | G | ⌊D⌋ | g | b | d | f | g | a | b | c♯ | d | e♭ |

[cfg   eab   gcd]

**270**

The origin of the main fundamental tones is explained by the fact that each one occurs as the third overtone of the one lying a fifth below it. So that C is the third overtone of F, just as G is the third overtone of C. In this manner $G:C = C:F$. And it is evident that C attracts the tones related to it through G, just as F and its related tones do with the complex of C.

The natural origin of these fundamentals of the main degrees, of the three main triads constructed on them, and of the resultant major scale from these components, as well as the circumstance that we actually to some extent hear and to some extent feel this relationship in every sounding tone, makes it possible for us to combine the tones of the major scale with one another.

2. But if we note the more distant overtones (up to the thirteenth) of these same fundamental tones, F, C, G, (see the table above) we find the chromatic scale. Thus there appear:

b♭ as the seventh overtone of C
f♯ " " eleventh " " C
e♭ " " seventh " " F and thirteenth of G
d♭ " " thirteenth " " F and eleventh of G
a♭ " " thirteenth " " C

**271**

Of course the lower overtones that lie nearer the fundamentals are more easily perceptible than the higher, more distant ones. It is certain that the more perceptible overtones sound more familiar to the ear than those it hears but faintly; these last therefore remain strange to it. For that reason the chromatic scale is a somewhat more complicated tonal form than the major. And since, moreover, the chromatic scale levels the differences in the intervals, a fundamental tone can hardly be regarded as implied at the outset. On the contrary the significance of the tones changes in accordance with the manner in which one or the other is artificially made the fundamental. In each case we have seven other major scale tones and five other non-diatonic tones. In the major scale the relation of the tones to one another is firm and constant through their relation to the fundamental, but in the chromatic scale the relation of the tones is variable and dependent entirely on whether one of the tones is regarded as a fundamental.

But let us bear in mind that the chromatic scale flows from the same source as the major: from the elements which are the constituents of every tone. The difference is only that the one imitates the natural sound up to the sixth overtone, while the other reaches about twice as far, to the thirteenth overtone; in other words, the chromatic scale brings the more distant overtones within the possibility of relationship.

And here is the answer to our question regarding the possibility of interconnection of the tones. It is founded on the fact that in the sounding tone and its nearest relative, the union and the companionship of the tones is continuously demonstrated to our ear, so that we do nothing more than imitate nature when we make use of these relations.

In the major scale the ear follows a clearly perceptible pattern. Other scales, as for example the minor and the church modes, I regard as art products. The church-modes represent, namely, previous attempts to find the true fundamental tone and its laws, whereas the minor scale has its particular characteristic less in the minor third than in the artificial imitation of the cadence, by means of a half step, which is found in the major scale.

**273**

The chromatic scale, as the result of the more distant overtones, raises the question whether, and by what means, one of its tones following or opposing its nature, may be made a fundamental; and we can only answer that the means must be the same as those employed in the major, which we shall examine more closely later. Of course, any tone of the chromatic scale can be made a fundamental if the succession of tone and chord combinations gives emphasis to such meaning. Each tone can pass for a fundamental if its most important characteristics are strengthened, for example, if its major third and its perfect fifth are reinforced, if the major triad which is lightly sounded in the overtone series be stressed, be awakened to life.

●

Not every succession of diatonic tones or chords unequivocally expresses a key, that is, the predominance of a fundamental tone. Every major triad by itself belongs to at least three major and three minor keys (and here we are not considering transitional dominants and the like). For instance the triad g-b-d belongs to C, G

**274**

and D-major as well as to A, E and B-minor. [See below, Example 1.] `

A succession of two chords, for example, V-I in C-major belongs to four keys (C and G-major, E and A-minor). [Example 2.]

But V-III in C-major belongs to six keys, namely C, G and D-major, and A. E and B-minor. [Example 3.]

Even a succession of four chords may belong to four keys, for instance, the succession III, VI, V, I of C-major may belong to C as well as to G, but also to E-minor and A-Minor. [Example 4.]

Anyone well versed in harmony knows that there are even more complicated instances and that tonality is often so endangered that one can only say "the last prevails." But in contradiction even to this, let me point to the B-flat Allegretto of Beethoven's *Eighth Symphony,*

**275**

where even the last does not prevail, for undoubtedly the piece does not end as it should in B-flat major, but rather on the V of E-flat major.

And this in spite of some of the cadences.

Cadences are successions of chords so chosen and arranged that a key appears to be set off from those it most resembles, and that its fundamental tone is significantly strengthened by being placed at the end.

But if the cadence were really a definite means to establish a key, we would not find, in the midst of a piece of music, cadences to various keys or degrees, the so-called modulations. And the classicists would not have been obliged to add many such cadences together if their feeling for form had not indicated that a key is not definately established through a cadence. Therefore the familiar endings, consisting of a number of cadences of various combinations are often further extended through repeated successions of V-I and concluding in several repetitions of I. Thus "the last prevails," a method of procedure which Wagner, as is known, ironically characterized as grandfatherly in "Papa Haydn." But unjustly so; for Haydn knew how difficult it is to set up a key definitely and how necessary such persistent emphasis was for apperception by his audience.

Even in the relatively simple forms, those most nearly related to the fundamental tone, which employ chords and chord successions that are very near the key, tonality does not appear automatically, of itself, but requires the application of a number of artistic means to achieve its end unequivocally and convincingly.

The question of endangering tonality becomes acute at that stage, where, in addition to the diatonic, key-determining chords, an excessive number of chords occur within a composition, whose use the key at best permits but which no longer definitely refer to it.

This danger manifested itself rather early in musical history. In my *Harmony-Treatise* I have shown how every diminished seventh-chord and every augmented triad belong to all major and minor keys and, what is more, in many a different sense. This is probably the place to point out that J. S. Bach in many "Introductions," for example, and especially such pieces or parts

**277**

labelled "Fantasia" prefers a disposition of the harmonic structure which neither in its entirety nor even in its detail can be easily referred to a key. It is not uninteresting that in just such instances these old masters use the name "Fantasia" and unconsciously tell us that fantasy, in contradistinction to logic, which everyone should be able to follow, favors a lack of restraint and a freedom in the manner of expression, permissible in our day only perhaps in dreams; in dreams of future fulfillment; in dreams of a possibility of expression which has no regard for the perceptive faculties of a contemporary audience; where one may speak with kindred spirits in the language of intuition and know that one is understood if one use the speech of the imagination—of fantasy.

To recapitulate :-

1.  Every isolated major triad can of itself express a key.
2.  If no contradiction is added it may be taken for a tonic-chord.
3.  But every succeeding chord contests the feeling for this tonality and pleads for others.

**278**

4. Only a few very special kinds of chord-successions permit the conception that any one of the used chords, chiefly the last one, is the fundamental chord of a key.

5. But even this designation is only final if nothing contradictory follows.

6. Without the application of very definite art-means a key cannot be unequivocally expressed.

For example: the last movement of Beethoven's quartet, Opus 59, No. 2 is in E-minor. We know this principally because it ends in E-minor. But it begins in C-major with a theme which uses every means to establish this key. After a few measures it turns to the key which Beethoven decides to make the main tonality of the piece. I beg you to give due consideration to this case: by every ingenious means C-major is at first stressed in the harmony and in the melody; and the subsequent turn to E-minor can be taken even at that point as the third degree of C-major. How unconvincing is a key under certain conditions, if such a group can still be taken as the main theme of a movement in E-minor! I could cite many

**279**

such instances in Beethoven, Brahms and other masters, where, in an extremely fine and ingenious manner, the ambiguity, that is, the indefiniteness of a key is made apparent.

We must conclude that neither at the beginning nor at the end, nor in the middle is the key automatically present. On the contrary at every point firm measures of art are required to give the key unequivocal expression.

Now then, since tonality is not something which the composer unconsciously achieves, which exists without his contribution and grows of itself, which would be present even if the composer willed the opposite; since, in a word, tonality is neither a natural nor automatic consequence of tone combinations and therefore cannot claim to be the automatic result of the nature of sound and so an indispensable attribute of every piece of music, we shall probably have to define tonality as the art of combining tones in such successions and such harmonies or successions of harmonies, that the relation of all events to a fundamental tone is made possible.

•

**280**

Thereupon the second question presents itself: Must tonality be unconditionally present in every piece of music?

To answer this, one might say that tonality could not be sacrificed.

1. if it accomplished the indispensable;
2. if no other substitute could be created for what it accomplishes.

Let us see what tonality accomplishes.

Even here the development of music can point the way. It is difficult to imagine that music could have pursued a road different from the one taken. Naturally at first the successions of the more directly related tones were obtained: the triad inherent in the tone, the major scale, the diatonic triads. It was natural also that these closely related results should be the first to be combined into forms.

But even here we find an inconsistency, a side-jump. For, strange to say, the near relationships were not realized immediately at the start, but only by the devious route of the church-modes. These reveal a remarkable phenomenon: the key of the underlying tonal series of

**281**

which they are composed is different from the key in which the piece really exists. If, for example, a piece is written in the Doric mode on D, the tones of which it is composed are those of C-major. But in this mode the tones d,e,f,g,a,b,c, should be related to the fundamental D, and all endings, all semi-cadences and all else that expresses the key should refer to this D. Naturally these tones, which are fixed by their intervals, with the leading tones e-f, and b-c, are without a doubt in the C-major tonality. As is well known, these seven tones are the material of other modes on E, F, G, etc. This contradiction was first resolved when the two principal modes used today were evolved out of the church-modes into a predominant position. Up to that time music can scarcely be regarded as tonal, in the present sense of the word. On the contrary we must concede that the church-modes do not at all conform to the law of tonality.

I have ventured to characterize the role played by the ear in the following statement: the presence of a fundamental tone was felt, but, since it was not known which of the scale tones possessed this quality, all tones were tried. However the opposite point of view might also be justified: it was felt that a fundamental could be present, but, since the necessity of allowing the claims of a particular tone was not demonstrated, all tones were tried. And, as a matter of fact, exactly this proved to be possible!

Let us hold to the essential results of the foregoing consideration:

1. Music at that time was without tonality as we understand it.

2. The tones of our major scale could be referred to different fundamentals from those predicated by our idea of tonality.

3. We arrived at our present-day tonality by a very roundabout process.

As the ear advanced to the major and minor tonality it was already inspired with the certainty that it was possible to add other tones to the seven diatonic ones generally used. The ear knew that in the series c,d,e,f,g,a,b, no matter what the mode, almost all the missing half-steps could be used as accidentals, namely: c-sharp and

**283**

b-flat in the Dorian mode, g-sharp in the Phrygian, b-flat in the Lydian, f-sharp in the Mixolydian, and g-sharp in the Aeolian,—all the tones except d-sharp, which appeared only later in transpositions. The major and minor tonalities were not based, as might be expected, from the beginning on seven diatonic tones, but included also the four or five non-diatonic tones, which not only served the chromaticism of melodies, but also the development of closed tonalities on the individual degrees, as I call them, or, as they are otherwise known, modulations to the nearest keys.

From the beginning major and minor tonalities were interspersed with non-diatonic elements tending to form opposition to the fundamental tone yet compelling the application of strong means in order to verify the tonality, to paralyze eccentric effects. This was evident even before Bach's time. The conflict becomes more acute in the Romantic period following the Classical. The increasing attraction exerted by foreign harmonies made them more and more a significant element of expression. I shall not adduce all the known facts, for everyone is

**284**

familiar today with the road that led from Schubert through Wagner to Reger, Richard Strauss, Mahler, Debussy and others. It is more important to state that this development began almost simultaneously with the realization of the major and minor tonalities, and that the art of music was never really in possession of a tonality wholly limited to the seven diatonic tones of the scale.

Though the development of tonality was by leaps and bounds, though it has not signified the identical thing at all times, its function has, nevertheless, been one and the same. It has always been the referring of all results to a centre, to a fundamental tone, to an emanation point of tonality, which rendered important service to the composer in matters of form. All the tonal successions, chords and chord-successions in a piece achieve a unified meaning through their definite relation to a tonal centre and also through their mutual ties.

That is the unifying function of tonality.

Just as important is its other, the articulating function, by means of which, parts that previously were unified by

**285**

a different application of the same means, are limited and separated. If, for example, a phrase in A-flat may on the one hand, be regarded as belonging to C-major, on the other, this A-flat is somewhat kindred to the original tonality, and its relationship though distant is nevertheless well balanced; in this manner it helps to produce what is required in every exposition of an idea: coherent contrast.

The degree of relationship allows a graduated removal of individual parts away from the tonal centre, according to the degree of their meaning: more remote digressions can thus be characterized differently from ideas that are closely related.

Not only the position of the parts but their form can be fixed by assistance of the tonality. Whether something be principal or subordinate idea, introduction or transition, episode, bridge, connecting link, embellishment, extension or reduction, whether independent or dependent, and, further, at which moment it begins or ceases to express one of these formal characteristics,—all this is possible for masters of form to make manifest through harmony. Characteristic kinds of beginnings and endings, basic and concentrated or resolving and liquidating dispositions of the harmony and many other means of art have accomplished that great clarity necessary to formal ends.

I perceive in both these functions, the conjoining and the unifying on the one hand, and on the other the articulating, separating, and characterizing, the main accomplishments of tonality. The resulting advantages to the composer and audience are as follows: through the unity of relationships, the listener of a certain degree of comprehension must inevitably perceive a work so composed to be a unit, to be a totality. On the other hand the impression on his memory is deepened by the articulating function which characteristically builds the whole and its parts as well as their relation to one another, thereby facilitating the comprehension of fugitive events. For instance the listener with a schooled musical ear will recognize the reprise of the theme through the return to the original key; he will also feel that so long as foreign keys are present the main theme is less likely to recur, but

**287**

rather secondary themes or developments. Such trained listeners have probably never been very numerous, but that does not prevent the artist from creating only for them.

It is evident that abandoning tonality can be contemplated only if other satisfactory means for coherence and articulation present themselves. If, in other words, one could write a piece which does not use the advantages offered by tonality and yet unifies all elements so that their succession and relation are logically comprehensible, and which is articulated as our mental capacity requires, namely so that the parts unfold clearly and characteristically in related significance and function.

Without a doubt there are means of accomplishing this; certainly it would not be impossible to mention and to explain at least a few. But our question, if we put it negatively, is easier to solve, and the answer can be given in a general, relevant form. Let us ask then: do unity and coherence depend exclusively on tonality? A few well known facts will quickly elucidate this question.

Everyone with a knowledge of music is aware that each

piece has certain parts, the smallest, which always recur: the so-called motives. Though it is not always possible or easy to follow the function of these motives in the most modern compositions, there is no doubt that it can almost always be done in the classics. The meaning of the elaboration of motives can only be uniformity (the more of an art-form the composition is, the most far-reaching the application): it is always the same material which is being handled; every form no matter where or how it appears may be traced back to these motives, the same idea is at the base of everything. Hence we shall find in the classics, besides the unity of tonal relations, that at least the same end of coherence is attained with at least the same amount of carefulness, through the unity of configurations, the unity of ideas.

Tonality is thus seen to be not the only means of producing the unity of a piece. It could, moreover, be easily shown that a work might have tonal unity, but nevertheless might still be confused in content, incoherent, superficial, external, yes, even without sense. It is apparent that it would not be difficult to apply to the harmonic

**289**

structure of any sonata movement of Beethoven—incoherently and without any connection—themes from his other works. That such a product would be sheer nonsense is obvious. It must of course be conceded that to attempt the reverse, to build a structure, moreover, artistic in its motive forms, but on a foundation harmonically senseless, would probably lead to just as unintelligent results.

But here I have been trying not to show how the greatest nonsense can be achieved, but rather, that harmony alone, while contributing essentially to unity and articulation cannot fill these requirements, since it needs other active art-means cooperating in the same direction. I am rather inclined to believe that one may sooner sacrifice logic and unity in the harmony, than in the thematic substance, in the motives, in the thought-content. Without doubt, in a genuine work of art, from the point of view of the ideal, there can be no serious consideration of the question as to whether one of the elements which compose it has less meaning than any other. Yet we know that dross is found in many a significant work. And if I reiterate that I do not regard tonality as the natural requirement of a piece of music, it will be understood in what sense I make the following statement:

It is difficult to conceive that a piece of music has meaning unless there is meaning in the motive and thematic presentation of ideas. On the other hand a piece whose harmony is not unified, but which develops its motive and thematic material logically, should, to a certain degree, have intelligent meaning. A message written in the worst orthography, with the grossest grammatical errors can nevertheless convey a clear, comprehensible report. On the other hand we know certain stylists, poets, who in recounting an incident are unable to state clearly, whether the lover shoots the husband or the wife, or whether the wife one of the others.

We have said that a meaningless harmonic foundation may support a structure artistic in its motive forms. If, even in this case, a certain effect cannot be denied the whole, how can it be denied when the harmony is not without meaning, when only the sense of the harmony is not easy to recognize, because, for example, certain requirements (tonality) are not fulfilled, or because it consists only of unresolved dissonances? It is obvious that such harmonies may appear irrational to an untrained ear which can just about receive the conventional. But there is no proof as yet that such a harmonic scheme lacks tonality, and it is easy to imagine that the concept of tonality will be so extended as to include all sorts of tone-combinations.

•

What detracts from the impression of tonality, according to my observation, is not so much the absence of the conventional formulae, the usual succession of degrees, that is, not alone the flow of these harmonies, but rather the appearance of a greater number of such tone successions and chords, the relation of which is difficult to account for, especially when their relation to a fundamental tone is not particularly emphasized.

This is the moment to consider the unresolved dissonances whose key relationship is not expressly fixed.

Up to a few decades ago only such chords were written as tended toward a key. These chords as a rule refer clearly to a fundamental, or they are made up of tones that have the melodic tendency to resolve like a leading tone, a half-step up or down; as, for example, the fourth-chords, which I have discussed in my *Harmony-Treatise.*

Distinct from these two groups is a great number of more-than-five-tone chords, the resolving tendencies of which have not as yet been systematically investigated. It can be maintained neither that they belong to a tonality, nor that they point toward one. And conversely neither can the opposite be held; no proof has yet been brought that these properties are entirely lacking. But something else can be proved. If, with the simplest triads, such as I have shown in the example above, we can produce short phrases which do not definitely determine a key, we can also take chords, not too complicated, such as are used in Wagner's harmony, and make rather extensive examples in which no unresolved dissonance occurs, all of which by themselves may refer to a key but which in toto leave no doubt that no tonal center exists and therefore no modulation. (Example 5)

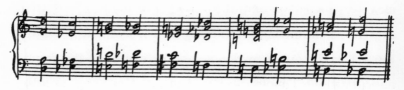

Then, too, conversely, we can take such chords as well as more complicated ones, that in no manner refer to a key, and join them to diatonic triads and similar successions, in this manner creating, *a posteriori,* an impression that the preceding dissonances, no matter how unprepared and unresolved, referred to this key.* (Example 6)

Strange to say, the ear accepts the final chord here just as it does a tonic and it might almost seem as if the preceding dissonances were really standing in legitimate relation to this tonic. The law mentioned before is again made manifest: "The last prevails."

One thing is certain: all chords, that in any way turn

*N. B.—Which of the two examples is tonal, which atonal?

to a key, no matter how dissonant they may be, fall within the domain of the old harmony and do not disturb tonality.

It might further be said:

Tonality does not depend on the number of dissonances used, nor on their eccentric effect, but rather

1 on whether these chords may be referred to a key; or

2 whether these relations are convincingly enough worked out.

Dissonances, even the simplest, are more difficult to comprehend than consonances. And therefore the battle about them goes on throughout the length of music history. The number of consonant chords is limited; in fact, it is rather small. The number of dissonances is so great that it would be difficult to systematize the relation of even the simplest ones to all the consonances and to each other, and to retain them in the memory. With the majority of dissonances the ear meets a new and unknown situation, often a situation for which there is not the slightest analogy. How difficult it was even with the four and five-tone dissonant chords for the hearer not to lose the sense of coherence! But as soon as the ear grew accustomed to such sounds and tonal combinations, recognizing old acquaintances, it learned also not to lose the coherence, even though the solution of the problem was revealed not immediately but later.

It is easier to recognize and define three different, simultaneously sounding tones than five or six; it is easier to follow and to perceive the succession of three, than of five or six. But is the use of polyphonic chords therefore unjustified because they are more difficult to apprehend?

*The criterion for the acceptance or rejection of dissonances is not that of their beauty, but rather only their perceptibility.* The recognition of coherence, logic, conclusiveness is one of the most important conditions for the apprehension of what occurs, and one can only understand what one has retained in memory. If $a$ plus $b$ equals $c$, I can conceive $c$ in the sense of $a$ plus $b$ only if I remember $a$ and $b$; only thus can I sum them up as equal to $c$. Since the presence of complicated dissonances does not necessarily endanger tonality, and since on the other

**296**

hand their absence does not guarantee it, we can ask now, what are the characteristics of that music which is today called "atonal." Permit me to point out that I regard the expression atonal as meaningless, and shall quote from what I have already expounded in detail in my treatise on Harmony. "Atonal can only signify something that does not correspond to the nature of tone." And further: "A piece of music will necessarily always be tonal in so far as a relation exists from tone to tone, whereby tones, placed next to or above one another, result in a preceptible succession. The tonality might then be neither felt nor possible of proof, these relations might be obscure and difficult to comprehend, yes, even incomprehensible. But to call any relation of tones atonal is as little justified as to designate a relation of colors aspectral or acomplementary. Such an antithesis does not exist."

I am usually not a coward; but if I should be asked to give this phenomenon a name, I would prefer—to avoid it entirely. But a habit has arisen of regarding music first, not with the ears by listening, second, not with the eyes by playing and reading it, and third, not with the mind but according to some technical peculiarity, for which there is a suitable slogan, a most striking term. "This symphony is impressionistic!" Yes, but has something occured to the writer? "This song is expressionistic!" Yes, but does the composer know anything? "This piano piece is atonal!" Yes, but does it contain an idea? And how is it accomplished? And what does the composer say that is new? or worth while saying?

If audiences and musicians would ask about these more important things and attempt to receive answers by listening, if further they would leave the idle talk and strife rather to the school-masters, who also must have something to do and wish to make a living, I, who have the hope that in a few decades audiences will recognize the *tonality* of this music today called *atonal*, would not then be compelled to attempt to point out any other difference than a *gradual* one between the tonality of yesterday and the tonality of today. Indeed, tonal is perhaps nothing else than what is understood *today* and atonal what will be understood in the *future*. In my *Har-*

*mony* treatise I have recommended that we give the term "pantonal" to what is called atonal. By this we can signify: the relation of all tones to one another, regardless of occasional occurrences, assured by the circumstance of a common origin.

I believe, to be sure, that this interrelationship of all tones exists not only because of their derivation from the first thirteen overtones of the three fundamental tones, as I have shown, but that, should this proof be inadequate, it would be possible to find another. For it is indisputable that we can join twelve tones with one another and this can only follow from the already existing relations between the twelve tones.

•

Now let us briefly recapitulate the assertions already advanced. Tonality has been revealed as no postulate of natural conditions, but as the utilization of natural possibilities; it is a product of art, a product of the technic of art. Since tonality is no condition imposed by nature, it is meaningless to insist on preserving it because of natural law. Whether, for artistic reasons, tonality must

**299**

be retained depends on whether it can be replaced. Since, as I have pointed out, the logical and artful construction of a piece of music is also secured by other means, and since the lack of tonality only increases the difficulty but does not exclude the possibility of comprehension; and since further proof of lack of tonality has not yet been adduced but as, on the contrary, probably much that to-day is not regarded as tonal, may soon be so accepted; and since dissonances need not in the least disturb tonality, no matter how increasingly difficult they may make the understanding of a work; and inasmuch as the use of exclusively tonal chords does not guarantee a tonal result, I come to the following conclusion: music which to-day is called "tonal" establishes a key relationship continuously or does so at least at the proper moment; but music which is today called "not tonal" never allows predominance of key relationships. The difference between the two methods is largely in the emphasis or non-emphasis on the tonality. We further conclude that the manner of composition of a piece abandoning tonality in the traditional sense must be different from that in which

**300**

tonality is followed. From this angle tonality is seen as *one of the means* which facilitates the unifying comprehension of a thought and satisfies the feeling for form. But since this means alone does not achieve the goal, it may be said that tonality accomplishes but a part of the purpose. If the function of tonality be dispensed with, but the same consideration be given to unity and feeling of form, this effect must be achieved by some other function. Obviously music so contrived can hardly be easy to grasp at the present time.

To prove the correctness of an idea no special method of order and construction in its presentation is demanded. The effort of the composer is solely for the purpose of making the idea comprehensible to the listener. For the latter's sake the artist must divide the whole into its parts, into surveyable parts, and then add them together again into a complete whole now conceivable in spite of hampering details. Experience teaches us that the understanding of the listener is an unstable quantity: it is not permanently fixed. Fortunately! It gradually accommodates itself to the demands made on it by the development of art. How otherwise would it have been possible, in scarcely more than sixty years, to follow the leaps and bounds of musical development that have led us from Wagner through Mahler, Reger, Strauss and Debussy to the harmony of today. Many are still living who can recall the difficulties presented to their sense-perception by the dissonances of Wagner. Certainly there must still be many today who only a short time ago found Mahler, Strauss, Reger and Debussy incomprehensible; yet today these composers must appear to them, at least in their manner of expression, self-evident. No longer does one lose the thread in their compositions — insofar as one holds it at all — because of incomprehensible harmonic passages. Nothing now hinders the understanding of their thoughts, the recognition of their melodies, of the flow and construction of their works. What at first appeared harmonically incoherent, wild, confused, arbitrary, eccentric and hideous is today felt to be beautiful.

If we imagine that the perceptive faculties of audiences will advance nearly as far in the near future as in those past years, then we must have faith that we shall achieve a true knowledge of the ideas presented today and an understanding of their beauty. The difficulty here is, in the first instance, to recognize and to feel in the polyphonic dissonant sounds, the capacity to be joined successively; to see in them elements of form and construction in the same manner as in the simple chords, and to feel also their relative measure of weight and significance just as in the older harmonies. Theoretical knowledge here is not the most essential need. Wagnerian and post-Wagnerian music was understood for a number of years before the derivation of certain chords and their relation to the key were theoretically established. Probably habit is all that is required; for it is able to prevent the recurrence of shock and the resultant lapse of presence of mind. He who is frightened is seldom in a position to follow exactly what is happening. Should such a one be accepted as witness, or rather one who does not lose presence of mind and remains calm, is enraptured or stirred only through the power of the idea and the emotion?

I do not assert that from now on there will be no more works of art which stress tonality; on the contrary, I believe that this is possible in more than one way. First, a popular art can exist beside pure art-music. Furthermore, works can be written occasionally ''in the old style.'' But I cannot deny the possibility that now, as often in the musical past, when harmony has developed to a certain high point, a change will occur which will bring with it entirely different and unexpected things. The best example of this we find in J. S. Bach, whose manner of composition was regarded as out-moded by his son, Philip Emanuel, and in whose time, directly at the apex of the contrapuntal style, the homophonic-melodic of the classical period began.

How such a new method of composition is to be contrived, I am as little in a position to say as probably Bach in his day. I hope it will not be held against me, if I confess that I have no faith in such an end—though I hold it to be possible. For the parallel is not entirely sound. Bach was, to be sure, the first and only one to found and develop a domain of contrapuntal writing. He carried over perfectly—a fact not yet discovered—the secret of the old contrapuntal art of former periods, from the church-modes to major and minor, from seven to twelve tones. This art had no predecessor and no successor and probably herein lies the explanation of the sudden turn toward a new goal; namely that the goal of the contrapuntal style had been perfectly realized! But the music of today is developing a field which must at first appear entirely new to us. And here probably is the difference: the field must first be cultivated. It is virgin soil. We are not at the high-point of an old art but rather at the beginning of a new one. It seems improbable to me that this is already the moment for departure; I do not believe we can afford to call a halt on work that is hardly begun; but naturally I am not able to dispute this.

Translated by ADOLPH WEISS

[1934]

**305**

# COMPOSITIONS

NOTE:—*Original Publisher: Richard Birnbach, Berlin,
　　　　　(formerly Dreililien)

　　　U.E.—Universal Edition
　　　B. & B.—Publishers Bote & Bock
　　　H.—　　　"　　　Hansen
　　　Heinr.—　　"　　　Heinrichshofen
　　　T. & J.　　　"　　　Tischer & Jagenberg

Op.　1—Two Songs for Piano and Baritone Voice*:
　　　　1.　Thanks (Levetzow) . . . . . . . . . . . . . . . . . . . . . . .U. E. 3650
　　　　2.　Farewell (Levetzow) . . . . . . . . . . . . . . . . . . . . . .U. E. 3651

Op.　2—Four Songs for Piano and Voice*:
　　　　1.　Expectation (Dehmel), middle range . . . . . . . . .U. E. 3652
　　　　2.　Give me thy golden comb (Dehmel), middle. . . .U. E. 3653
　　　　3.　Exaltation (Dehmel), high range . . . . . . . . . . . . .U. E. 3654
　　　　4.　The Forest Sun (Schlaf), high . . . . . . . . . . . . . . .U. E. 3655

Op.　3—Six Songs for Piano and Voice*, middle range:
　　　　1.　George von Frundsberg (from "The Youth's
　　　　　　　Magic Horn") . . . . . . . . . . . . . . . . . . . . . . . .U. E. 3656
　　　　2.　The Excited Ones (Keller) . . . . . . . . . . . . . . . . .U. E. 3657
　　　　3.　The Warning (Dehmel) . . . . . . . . . . . . . . . . . . .U. E. 3658
　　　　4.　The Wedding Song (J. P. Jacobson). . . . . . . . . .U. E. 3659
　　　　5.　An Experienced Heart (G. Keller) . . . . . . . . . . .U. E. 3660
　　　　6.　Free and Fair (Lingg) . . . . . . . . . . . . . . . . . . . .U. E. 3661

Op.　4—String sextet "Transfigured Night"* for
　　　　　2 violins, 2 violas, 2 violoncelli:
　　　　Score . . . . . . . . . . . . . . . . . . . . . . . . . . . . . . . . . . . .U. E. 3662
　　　　Voices . . . . . . . . . . . . . . . . . . . . . . . . . . . . . . . . . . . .U. E. 3663
　　　　Version for string orchestra (U. E.) Score. . . . . . . .U. E. 6065

# 307

**Op. 8**—(Continued).

    6.  When little birds make their plaint
          (Petrarca), high range, score . . . . . . . . . . . .U. E. 5286
          Edition for piano and voice (Webern) . . . . . . . .U. E. 3046

**Op. 9**—Chamber Symphony in E-major for fifteen
        solo instruments (U. E.) score . . . . . . . . . . . . . . . .U. E. 3667
        Study score . . . . . . . . . . . . . . . . . . . . . . . . . . . . . . . . . . . .U. E. 7147
        Piano arrangement (Steuermann) . . . . . . . . . . . . . . .U. E. 7146
        Piano arrangement, 4 hands (Greissle) . . . . . . . . . .U. E. 7502
        Thematic analysis (Alban Berg) . . . . . . . . . . . . . . . .U. E. 6140
        (also edition for grand salon)
        The same, arrangement for flute (or 2 violins),
          clarinet (or viola), violin, violoncello and piano
        by Anton Webern (in copy)

**Op. 9b**—Chamber Symphony
        Version for full orchestra (1935), G. Schirmer, Inc.

**Op. 10**—Second string quartet F-sharp minor,
        2 violins, viola and violoncello;
        Third and Fourth movement with songs of poems
          by Stefan Georg (U. E.) score . . . . . . . . . . . . . . . .U. E. 2993
        Voices . . . . . . . . . . . . . . . . . . . . . . . . . . . . . . . . . . . . . . . . .U. E. 2994
        Piano arrangement for 4 hands (Greissle) . . . . . . . .U. E. 7179
        **Excerpts:**
        Third movement, "Litany," for piano
          and voice (Alban Berg) . . . . . . . . . . . . . . . . . . . . . . .U. E. 6862
        Fourth movement, "Rapture," for piano
          and voice (Alban Berg) . . . . . . . . . . . . . . . . . . . . . . .U. E. 6863
        The same, transcription for string orchestra, score..U. E. S.33

**Op. 11**—Three Pianoforte Pieces (U. E.) . . . . . . . . . . . . . . .U. E. 2991

**Op. 11**—Second Pianoforte Piece. Concert version
        by Feruccio Busoni (U. E.) . . . . . . . . . . . . . . . . . . . .U. E. 2992

**311**

Op. 24—(Continued).

Study score . . . . . . . . . . . . . . . . . . . . . . . . . . . . . . . . . . . E. H. 2400

Version for piano, violin and cello . . . . . . . . . . . . . . E. H. 2455

Fourth movement: Sonnet No. 217 by Petrarca,
arrangement for a bass-baritone voice, piano com-
position by Felix Greissle . . . . . . . . . . . . . . . . . . E. H. 2403

Op. 25—Dance Suite for Piano (U. E.) . . . . . . . . . . . . . . . . . U. E. 7627

Op. 26—Quintet for flute, oboe, clarinet, fagotte, and horn
(U. E.) Score . . . . . . . . . . . . . . . . . . . . . . . . . . . . . . U. E. 7668

Voices . . . . . . . . . . . . . . . . . . . . . . . . . . . . . . . . . . . . . U. E. 7669

Piano duet (arrangement for four hands)
(Greissle) . . . . . . . . . . . . . . . . . . . . . . . . . . . . . . . U. E. 7670

Sonnet, following quintet of wind instruments for
violins, (or flute) and piano (Greissle) . . . . . . . U. E. 8375

Sonnet, following quintet of wind instruments for
clarinet and piano (Greissle) . . . . . . . . . . . . . . . U. E. 8376

Op. 27—Four Compositions for Mixed Choir:
(U. E.) Score . . . . . . . . . . . . . . . . . . . . . . . . . . U. E. 8549

1. Inescapable (a cappella, text by Arnold
Schönberg)

2. You shall not, you must! (a cappella text by
Arnold Schönberg)

3. The Moon and Mortals (a cappella from
"The Chinese Flute")

4. The Lover's Wish (from "The Chinese Flute,"
with mandoline, clarinet, violin and 'cello)

Op. 28—Three Satires for Mixed Choir (U. E.)
Text by Arnold Schönberg. Score . . . . . . . . . . . U. E. 8586

1. At the Parting of the Way (a capp.)

2. Manysided (a capp.)

3. The New Classicism.

Op. 28—(Continued).

A small cantata with viola, cello and piano.—
Appendix: 1. A citation and two variations on
it. 2. Canon for string quartet. 3. Sanctification of canon (for Bernard Shaw's 70th
birthday).

Op. 29—Suite:
1. Overture,
2. Dance steps,
3. Theme and variations,
4. Gigue
for piano, small clarinet, clarinet, bass-
clarinet, violin, viola and violoncello (U. E.)
Score and voices . . . . . . . . . . . . . . . . . . . . . . . . U. E. 8685
Score alone

Op. 30—Third string quartet for 2 violins, viola, violoncello
(U. E.) Score . . . . . . . . . . . . . . . . . . . . . . . . . . . . U. E. 8927
Voices . . . . . . . . . . . . . . . . . . . . . . . . . . . . . . . . . . . U. E. 8928

Op. 31—Variations for orchestra (U. E.) Score . . . . . . . . . . . U. E. 9614

Op. 32—From Today to Tomorrow. Opera in one act by
Max Blonda (U. E.),
Piano arrangement with text . . . . . . . . . . . . . . . . U. E. 10.545

Op. 33a—Piano piece (U. E.) . . . . . . . . . . . . . . . . . . . . . . . U. E. 9773

Op. 34—Accompaniment to a film show
(Pressing danger, fear, catastrophe) for orchestra
(Heinr.), Score

Op. 35—Six pieces for male choir a cappella (B. & B.), Score
Voices

Op. 36—Concerto for violin and orchestra (1936)

**313**

Op. 37—Fourth string quartet (1936)
Unfinished
Jacob's Ladder, oratorio
Moses and Aron, opera

## WORKS WITHOUT OPUS NUMBERS

Gurre Songs (Group of Love Songs).
(Jens Peter Jacobsen). For solo voice, choir and full or-
chestra (U. E.) Score . . . . . . . . . . . . . . . . . . . . . . . . . . . . U. E. 6300
Study score (Facsimile reproduction of original manu-
script of score) . . . . . . . . . . . . . . . . . . . . . . . . . . . . . . . . . . U. E. 3697
Piano arrangement with text (Alban Berg) . . . . . . . . . . . U. E. 3696
Guide (Alban Berg), small edition . . . . . . . . . . . . . . . . . . . U. E. 3695
Guide (Alban Berg), large edition . . . . . . . . . . . . . . . . . . . U. E. 5275
Single Editions for Piano and Voice:
Waldemar's Song "Thus the angels dance," high . . . . . . . . . U. E. 5330
Tove's Song "I tell thee for the first time," high . . . . . . . . . U. E. 5331
Waldemar's Song "Thou wonderful Tove," high range . . . . U. E. 5332
Song of the Forest-Dove "Doves of Gurre," middle . . . . . . . U. E. 5333

Song of the Forest Dove from the Gurre-Songs, middle range,
for voices and orchestra (also version for small orchestra
and for chamber-orchestra) (U. E.)
Score (Arrangement for chamber-orchestra) . . . . . . . . . . . U. E. 7272
Edition for piano and voice . . . . . . . . . . . . . . . . . . . . . . . . U. E. 5333

Texts:

Introduction
Death dance of Principles
Requiem
Jacob's Ladder
The Lucky Hand
(U. E.), complete in one volume . . . . . . . . . . . . . . . . . . . . . U. E. 7731

Single Editions:

Jacob's Ladder, oratorio (U. E.) . . . . . . . . . . . . . . . . . . . . . U. E. 6061
The same, Buetten-edition . . . . . . . . . . . . . . . . . . . . . . U. E. 6061a

## 314

The Lucky Hand, drama with music (U. E.) . . . . . . . . . . . . . U. E. 5672

Third Manual on Harmony,
 revised and appended edition (U. E.). . . . . . . . . . . . . . . . . . . U. E. 3370

Piano Piece (printed in magazine "New Music," 1932)

Concerto for violoncello and orchestra (1932) (based on the
 Concerto for clavicombalo, composed in 1746 by Josef
 Matthias Monn, 1717-1750) (G. Schirmer, Inc.)

Concerto for string quartet and orchestra (1933) (based on
 the Concerto Grosso opus 6 No. 7 by G. F. Handel)
 (G. Schirmer, Inc.)

Suite for string orchestra (1934) (G. Schirmer, Inc.)

MUSICAL ARRANGEMENTS
TRANSCRIPTIONS

J. S. Bach: Two Choral Preludes for organ, for large orchestra, transcribed by Arnold Schönberg (U. E.)
 1. Come, Lord, Creator, Holy Ghost, Score . . . . . . . . . . . U. E. 7648
 2. Enhance thyself, oh lovely soul, Score . . . . . . . . . . . U. E. 7650

J. S. Bach: Prelude and Fugue, E-major for organ, for large
 orchestra, transcribed by Arnold Schönberg (U. E.),
 Score . . . . . . . . . . . . . . . . . . . . . . . . . . . . . . . . . . . . . . . . . . . . . U. E. 9876

M. G. Monn: Concerto for violoncello in G-minor, with
 string orchestra and cembalo. Arrangement by Arnold
 Schönberg (U. E.), Edition for violoncello and piano . . . . . U. E. 5351

Carl Loewe: Ballad, "The Noeck." Orchestral accompaniment by Arnold Schönberg (in copy) (U. E.)

Folk Songs—Arrangements:
 Three Choirs,
 Five Songs for solo voice and piano,
 (In the collection of Folk-Songs of the Prussian Ministry
 of Education, 1929).

**315**

# ACKNOWLEDGMENTS

Acknowledgment is made to the following individuals and publications for material listed below:

Music in Crisis . . . . . . . . . Roger Sessions
Modern Music, Jan.-Feb., 1933.

Problems of Harmony . . . . . Arnold Schoenberg
(Translated by Adolph Wiess) Modern Music, May-June, 1934.

Arnold Schoenberg . . . . . . Ernst Krenek, 1934
(Translated by Christel Gang.)

Schoenberg's Compositions
(Translated by Christel Gang.)

The Truth About Schoenberg . . . César Saerchinger
Musical Courier, Jan. 11, 1930.

Schoenberg's Twelve-Tone Operas . Paul Amadeus Pisk
Modern Music, April-May, 1930.

**317**

The Way of Understanding . . . . Boris de Schloezer
Modern Music, April-May, 1930.

Tonality and Form . . . . . . Arnold Schoenberg
Pacific Coast Musician, May 4, 1935.

Schoenberg's Operas . . . . . . . . Paul Stefan
Modern Music, Dec.-Jan., 1929-30.

Affirmations . . . . . The New York Herald-Tribune
Sept. 17, 1933 and Oct. 31, 1933.
Article by Jerome D. Bohm, Sept. 17, 1933.
The Music News, Feb. 16, 1934.
Musical Courier (Vienna), March 13, 1933.
The New York Times, Oct. 22, 1933.
Statement to David Ewen.

"Tribute" by Franz Werfel and
"Schoenberg's Sound" by Erwin Stein from
"Arnold Schoenberg Sixtieth Birthday Book."

The Twelve-Tone Series . . . . . . Adolph Weiss
Modern Music, March-April, 1932.

**318**

The foreword by Leopold Stokowski, and the articles by Merle Armitage, Ernst Krenek, Richard Buhlig, Eduard Steuermann, José Rodriguez, Carl Engel, Berthold Viertel, Otto Klemperer, Louis Danz and Nicholas Slonimsky were written especially for this book.

The portrait photographs by Edward Weston, the two ink drawings by Carlos Dyer as well as the drawing on the end papers were made for this volume, as were the candid camera photographs by Otto Rothschild.

A major contribution in research and revision was made by Ramiel McGehee.

319

PORTRAIT BY GEORGE GERSHWIN

PORTRAIT BY EDWARD WESTON

PORTRAIT BY EDWARD WESTON

MANUSCRIPTS IN FACSIMILE OF
LATEST SCHOENBERG OPUS
(ON TWO FOLLOWING PAGES)

S E L F  P O R T R A I T  (1910)

SCHOENBERG REHEARSING
CANDID CAMERA PHOTOGRAPH BY OTTO ROTHSCHILD

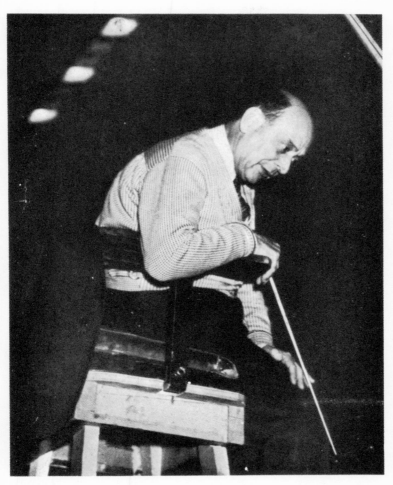

## SCHOENBERG REHEARSING
CANDID CAMERA PHOTOGRAPH BY OTTO ROTHSCHILD